DECODING AUTISM

and

LEADING *the* WAY *to* SUCCESSFUL INCLUSION

DECODING AUTISM

and

LEADING the WAY to SUCCESSFUL INCLUSION

Barbara Boroson

Alexandria, Virginia USA

1703 N. Beauregard St. • Alexandria, VA 22311-1714 USA
Phone: 800-933-2723 or 703-578-9600 • Fax: 703-575-5400
Website: www.ascd.org • E-mail: member@ascd.org
Author guidelines: www.ascd.org/write

Ranjit Sidhu, *CEO & Executive Director;* Stefani Roth, *Publisher;* Genny Ostertag, *Director, Content Acquisitions;* Allison Scott, *Acquisitions Editor;* Julie Houtz, *Director, Book Editing & Production;* Katie Martin, *Editor;* Judi Connelly, *Senior Art Director;* Donald Ely, *Associate Art Director;* Keith Demmons, *Senior Production Designer;* Kelly Marshall, *Manager, Production Services;* Isel Pizarro, *Senior Production Specialist;* Shajuan Martin, *E-Publishing Specialist*

All web links in this book are correct as of the publication date below but may have become inactive or otherwise modified since that time. If you notice a deactivated or changed link, please e-mail books@ascd.org with the words "Link Update" in the subject line. In your message, please specify the web link, the book title, and the page number on which the link appears.

PAPERBACK ISBN: 978-1-4166-2919-1   ASCD product #118008   n8/20
PDF E-BOOK ISBN: 978-1-4166-2921-4; see Books in Print for other formats.
Quantity discounts are available: e-mail programteam@ascd.org or call 800-933-2723, ext. 5773, or 703-575-5773. For desk copies, go to www.ascd.org/deskcopy.

Library of Congress Cataloging-in-Publication Data

Names: Boroson, Barbara, author.
Title: Decoding autism and leading the way to successful inclusion /
  Barbara Boroson.
Description: Alexandria, Virginia : ASCD, 2020. | Includes bibliographical
  references and index.
Identifiers: LCCN 2020014021 (print) | LCCN 2020014022 (ebook) | ISBN
  9781416629191 (paperback) | ISBN 9781416629214 (pdf)
Subjects: LCSH: Children with autism spectrum disorders--Education--United
  States. | Autism spectrum disorders in children. | Inclusive
  education--United States.
Classification: LCC LC4718 .B673 2020 (print) | LCC LC4718 (ebook) | DDC
  371.94--dc23
LC record available at https://lccn.loc.gov/2020014021
LC ebook record available at https://lccn.loc.gov/2020014022

29 28 27 26 25 24 23 22 21 20   1 2 3 4 5 6 7 8 9 10 11 12

DECODING AUTISM
and LEADING the WAY to SUCCESSFUL INCLUSION

Introduction

Inclusion is a hallmark of contemporary education in the United States. Today's public school classrooms are more diverse than ever before, and curriculum is infused with myriad new sensibilities and sensitivities. And it's a good thing, too, because in recent decades, the prevalence of autism has skyrocketed, bringing profound new challenges to the education community.

Generally speaking, the more diverse and inclusive our classrooms and schools are, the more robust and rewarding the learning environment becomes. But it must also be noted that the more diverse and inclusive our classrooms and schools are, the more often education leaders like you will find someone knocking at your door with a question or concern. That very same diversity that greatly benefits students, schools, and districts requires knowledgeable and mindful support from superintendents, assistant superintendents, principals, assistant principals, teacher leaders, and others in and around the school community. Inclusion of students on the autism spectrum in the classroom asks a lot of your teachers; it can make teaching harder. You're going to have to give them all the help you can.

Many students on the spectrum bring with them an array of distinct strengths and quirky expertise that add intriguing new dimensions to an educational program. But they can also bring with them challenges that are broader, deeper, and more idiosyncratic and intractable than those of their typically developing peers.

As a leader, you set the tone; you spread the gospel. It's up to you to share and promote a detailed and nuanced understanding of autism spectrum disorder (ASD). It's up to you to determine whether these students are welcomed, supported, understood, and therefore successful or . . . well . . . *not*. It's up to you to ensure that every single member of the faculty and staff—from teachers and paraeducators to every secretary, custodian, lunch aide, and recess monitor—is on board and up to speed on inclusion and ASD. And it's up to me—through this book—to give you information you need to lead this charge competently, confidently, and compassionately.

This book is intended to help you "decode" the many manifestations of ASD and lead educators to attend to the individual needs of students on the autism spectrum in the context of the whole classroom and the whole school. That's what inclusive education is all about. Within these pages you will learn about the particular challenges that students on the spectrum face and collect preventive and responsive strategies that you and your faculty and staff can use efficiently and effectively.

Decoding Autism and Leading the Way to Successful Inclusion is best read cover-to-cover, as the chapters combine to provide a holistic view of ASD and help you develop new ways of seeing and being in and around your school and district. But after you've taken it all in, come back to specific chapters as needed for a quick brush-up on what's happening, why it's happening, and what you can do about it.

Here's what you'll find in the pages ahead:

Chapter 1, "Autism Spectrum Disorder Today," reviews the evolution of the diagnosis and its current prevalence. We will also look at federal regulations governing the education of students with disabilities and at inclusive and other options for education settings and interventions.

Having set the stage, we will turn our attention to decoding specific areas of challege, summarizing each one's etiology and describing its manifestation. Then each chapter goes on to provide strategies for pre-empting, addressing, and ameliorating that challenge and leading the way to successful inclusion.

Chapter 2, "Anxiety," explains why anxiety is a baseline emotional state for students on the autism spectrum. Here you will gain important insight into how to avoid common exacerbating triggers and learn to respect the power of the comfort anchor.

Chapter 3, "Executive Function," demonstrates that difficulties in executive function can affect almost every aspect of students' experience in classroom settings in big ways. In this chapter you will gather strategies to help students and their teachers regulate actions and reactions and avoid total system failure.

Chapter 4, "Sensation," explores the complicated world of sensory modulation and other sensory factors that are intense triggers for most students on the spectrum. Here, you will get a sense of the variable effects that sensation has on these students and the distinctive ways they try to self-regulate, and you will collect strategies to help you and their teachers ease their way.

Chapter 5, "Communication and Socialization," speaks to the ever-present communication and social challenges that typify ASD, many of which relate to pragmatic language. This chapter looks at fundamental communication and social challenges. The strategies it provides will help teachers maximize the efficacy of social-emotional learning for students on the spectrum and help you lead a cadre of supporters throughout your school community.

Chapter 6, "Engagement and Cognitive Acquisition," digs into the inner workings of the autistic mind. Why can these students seem so far away? How can teachers reel them in, ready to learn? Here you will find creative and sometimes counterintuitive classroom strategies for reaching and teaching these students and getting them hooked into curricular learning.

Chapter 7, "Behavior," comes relatively and perhaps surprisingly late in the book—with good reason. Once you and your faculty and staff have developed a deeper understanding of what students on the spectrum are communicating via their actions and reactions (as explained in Chapters 2–6), you'll encounter far fewer disruptive behaviors. However, when they do occur, Chapter 7 is here to provide guidance on how best to respond.

Chapter 8, "Parents and Guardians," examines the perspectives of these essential members of the school community, providing insights as to why relationships with them can be so fraught and how you can lead the way to more productive collaboration.

This book taps into the dual perspectives of its author. I have been a school administrator, autism educator, clinician, and consultant for almost 30 years, and I'm also a parent of a young adult on the autism spectrum. My combination of professional and personal experience infuses my books with a deep understanding of individuals on the spectrum as multifaceted people who are imbued with skills, talents, and knowledge right alongside their considerable challenges.

It is difficult to present the autism spectrum as a single entity while still doing justice to the differentness of the individuals who are on that spectrum. Fact is, there is no way to generalize as to which "kinds" of students on the spectrum will do better in inclusion classrooms, or what "types" will fare better in special classes. There is no such thing as being on "one end of the spectrum" or another. And common categorizations such as high- and low-functioning autism seriously miss the mark. Here's why: Imagine an actual visual light spectrum—picture it in your mind. Does red, at one end, mean "least colorful" and violet, at the other, mean "most colorful"? No. That would be a gradient, not a spectrum (Lynch, 2019). Instead, consider that different locations on a color spectrum represent more of some kinds of light and less of others. Some students on the autism spectrum have significant social challenges but are not easily triggered by sensation. Some may be cognitively strong while exhibiting flagrant self-stimulatory behaviors. Others may be highly verbal while also quite difficult to engage. They are all on the spectrum, each exhibiting a personal and unique composition of shades and hues, light and shadow. (Read more about the inaccuracy of the terms *high-* and *low-functioning* in Chapter 1.)

An inclusive school must support and educate students with identified disabilities alongside their typical peers to the greatest extent possible. In an inclusive school, students with special needs are placed in a variety of classroom environments but are all recognized as equally valuable members of the school community and are actively considered and included in all school and districtwide events to the greatest extent possible. This is the essence of inclusive education and reflects the spirit of least restricted environment (LRE) as described in the Individuals with Disabilities Education Act (IDEA). This also means that some of the students on the spectrum in your inclusion classes will be bright red with very little blue; others, deep violet with hints of yellow and green; and others, representing every color of the rainbow.

Some students on the spectrum unequivocally do need the all-encompassing, autism-adapted environment that a special class setting or special program can provide. However, many can flourish in an inclusion classroom where they can learn and socialize right alongside their typically developing peers—as long as they get the modifications, accommodations, and differentiated instruction they need. When inclusive programming is done well, every student in the building, as well as every adult member of the school community, stands to grow and benefit from the experience. For most students on the spectrum, an inclusive school is not only the least restrictive environment—it's also the *best* environment.

In this book, I generally refer to students who have autism spectrum disorder as being "on the spectrum." I use this terminology to reinforce the concept that autism spectrum disorder is really not one single entity but an endless array of color gradations, each luminescent and different from the next. There are so many variations, in fact, that it is impossible—and inaccurate—to paint the entire spectrum with a single brush. On the one hand, an individual who is nonverbal, nonambulatory, and incontinent may be considered to be on the autism spectrum. On the other hand, Dan Aykroyd, Tim Burton, Emily Dickinson, Stanley Kubrick, Nikola Tesla, Greta Thunberg, Alan Turing, and Andy Warhol also may be considered to be on the autism spectrum. All of these people are believed to meet the criteria of a single diagnosis: autism spectrum disorder. That's why I put an emphasis on the *spectrum.*

Another word about inclusive words: while this book focuses primarily on inclusion as it relates to the education of students on the autism spectrum in a co-taught classroom, inclusion is also a state of mind. A *diverse* school and an *inclusive* school are two very different things. A diverse school is one that contains students of many different races, cultures, religions, genders, orientations, and abilities, all coexisting —peacefully or otherwise. An inclusive school is a unified community composed of all of those students—as well as their families, teachers, support staff, and leaders— and is built on a framework of mutual understanding, respect, and support for all individuals. To that end, this book seeks to use exclusively inclusive language. This includes, in part, the use of the singular *they, them,* and *their* to be inclusive of students who are nonbinary, questioning, or otherwise gender fluid.

My hope is that by the time you reach the end of this book, you will have a deeper appreciation of the many hues of ASD and a better sense of inclusion as the differentiated unifier that it is. When you hear that knock on your door, buzz of your phone, or ping of a new message, you will be ready to welcome all comers with competence, confidence, and compassion.

Autism Spectrum Disorder Today

It's not your imagination: there are more students on the autism spectrum in our schools now than ever before. That's because autism is being diagnosed more now than ever before. Whereas in 2000, 1 in every 150 children in the United States had a diagnosis of an autism spectrum disorder, by 2018 the U.S. Centers for Disease Control (CDC) confirmed that the prevalence had reached 1 in every 59 children (Baio et al., 2018). The clear question is *why*. The answer, however, is not a straightforward one, and the factors are anything but clear.

In this chapter, we will take a look at the increasing prevalence and evolving definition of autism and at what regulations and options guide educational program provision today.

Decoding the Diagnosis

One likely explanation for the increase in the number of students on the autism spectrum is the changing clinical definition of autism over the years. As the diagnostic terms have broadened, more and more students are meeting the criteria for autism diagnosis.

How Did We Get Here?

Before 1994, autistic disorder could be diagnosed in an individual only when highly significant impairments in the areas of social interaction, communication, and behavior were manifest. These criteria restricted the diagnosis to individuals who were deeply lost in themselves: most either nonverbal or minimally verbal, often profoundly idiosyncratic or mercurial in their interactions and behavior, and quite limited in self-care abilities.

Asperger's In

In 1994, when the American Psychiatric Association published the fourth edition of the *Diagnostic and Statistical Manual of Mental Disorders* (DSM-IV), autistic disorder was subsumed into a broad category called pervasive developmental disorders (PDD). DSM-IV identified five subtypes of PDD: Rett's syndrome, childhood disintegrative disorder, autistic disorder, Asperger's syndrome, and pervasive development disorder–not otherwise specified (PPD-NOS).

At that time, the newly defined subtype called Asperger's syndrome differed in significant ways from the other PDD subtypes. While individuals with an Asperger's syndrome diagnosis presented social idiosyncrasies and restricted, repetitive patterns of behavior much like their peers elsewhere on the autism spectrum, they did not present delayed or impaired speech. Additionally, most individuals with Asperger's presented relatively better-developed cognitive, adaptive, and self-help skills. They were generally articulate, somewhat independent, at or near grade level academically, and relatively ready to learn. Before DSM-IV, these relative strengths would have precluded this cohort of students from meeting the criteria for any kind of autism diagnosis.

Did students like these exist prior to 1994? They sure did. Some were never officially identified or diagnosed at all; they slipped under the diagnostic radar, often thought of as "quirky kids" or "little professors." Others were diagnosed with a learning disability or emotional disturbance, or classified as "other health impaired," for lack of a more suitable moniker. The subtype Asperger's syndrome filled a need for a more descriptive diagnosis for these students who didn't quite meet the earlier criteria for autistic disorder, and it paved the way for them to receive much-needed social, behavioral, and other services both in and out of school.

Asperger's Out

In the fifth edition of the *Diagnostic and Statistical Manual of Mental Disorders* (DSM-5), published in 2013, the criteria for diagnosing autism-related symptomatology changed once again. Experts had begun to suspect that the five subtypes of pervasive developmental disorders were insufficiently distinguishable from one another.

They feared that subjectivity was interfering with diagnosis and perhaps contributing to the sharp rise in diagnostic rates. To that end, all five subtypes have been absorbed back into a single umbrella term with a broader reach: *autism spectrum disorder* (ASD). To reduce the unreliability of subjective interpretation, diagnosticians now substantiate and justify an ASD diagnosis by completing standardized rating scales and providing annotative descriptions that characterize the specific nature of an individual's functioning. Anyone who would have met the former criteria for any of the PDD subtypes would now be diagnosed, simply, with ASD (American Psychological Association [APA], 2013).

Although there were a number of contentious components related to this change, the most enduring controversy surrounds the elimination of Asperger's syndrome as a diagnosis. During the 19 years in which it was an active diagnosis, many individuals who were diagnosed with Asperger's syndrome—my own son among them—took some degree of comfort in having a specific diagnosis that clearly distinguished them from their more profoundly affected peers on the autism spectrum. Those who grew comfortable with their Asperger's diagnosis may be loath to renounce that signifier— and they don't have to. Even though Asperger's syndrome and other PDD subtypes are no longer being diagnosed, individuals who received those diagnoses previously are free to continue using them.

As the diagnostic criteria have evolved and broadened over the last 25 years, more and more individuals, whose challenges might once have been only vaguely recognized, now find a home on the autism spectrum. From this perspective, the skyrocketing "prevalence" rates may more reflect the broadening and redefining of the diagnosis than an increase in the actual incidence of autism.

Co-Incidentally . . .

Scientific theories abound as to whether there is *also* an increase in the actual incidence of autism, and if so, why.

One such theory regarding the etiology of ASD is gaining traction. Genetic markers have been identified that change the way instructions in the genetic code are translated and carried out by the body. These changes, known as *mosaic mutations*, may alter the nature of a gene's expression. Depending on the way these markers interact with other genes and with the environment, they may predispose a child to be genetically more susceptible to having ASD (Krupp et al., 2017).

The Vaccine-Autism Fallacy

The global vaccine fallacy perpetrated by discredited doctor Andrew Wakefield has now been completely debunked by science. His broadly accepted but baseless claim linking vaccines to autism had been published in the scientific journal *The Lancet* in 1998. However, in 2010, upon finding that the study was undermined by falsified data, ethical violations, and financial conflicts of interest, *The Lancet* unequivocally renounced and retracted Wakefield's claims, and the British General Medical Council stripped him of his license to practice medicine. Since then, study after study conducted by unbiased researchers has shown absolutely no association between vaccines and autism. The *Washington Post* stated plainly, "First things first: 'Vaccines do not cause autism.' So says the Centers for Disease Control and Prevention, the World Health Organization, the National Academies of Sciences, Engineering and Medicine, and the American Academy of Pediatrics, along with dozens of studies published in prestigious, peer-reviewed journals. The scientific consensus on vaccines and autism is thorough and solid: There is no evidence of a connection" (Kaplan, 2017). Indeed, the American Academy of Pediatrics has produced a 21-page document containing summaries and links to dozens of studies and reports that demonstrate the safety of vaccines (2018).

But, regrettably, the damage was done. This false connection has been extremely hard to shake in public perceptions about autism. You will surely encounter parents who remain convinced that vaccines are to blame for their children's autism, and other parents who eschew vaccinations altogether for this reason.

Please spread the facts: ASD is neurodevelopmental in nature, meaning that it is related to the wiring of the brain, and it manifests during the early years of child development—the same years when most vaccines are administered. However, the use of vaccines during that developmental period is coincidental, not causal. Autism is not caused by vaccines.

What Is Autism Spectrum Disorder Today?

According to the DSM-5 (APA, 2013), in order to qualify for the diagnosis of ASD, individuals must meet, across multiple contexts, *all* of the five criteria described in Figure 1.1.

Figure 1.1: Practical Summary of Autism Diagnosis

Criteria	Common Components	Examples of What to Look For
1. Persistent deficits in social communication and social interaction, not accounted for by general developmental delays.	• Deficits in social-emotional reciprocity. • Deficits in nonverbal communicative behaviors. • Deficits in developing and maintaining relationships beyond those with caregivers.	• Atypical social approach, failure of expectable back-and-forth conversation, reduced sharing of interests and emotions. • Poorly integrated verbal and nonverbal communication; atypical eye contact and body language; limited of understanding or use of facial expression and gestures. • Difficulties adjusting behavior to suit different social contexts; difficulty sharing imaginative play, making friends; apparent lack of interest in peers.
2. Restricted, repetitive patterns of behavior, interests, or activities.	• Stereotyped or repetitive speech, motor movements, or use of objects. • Rigid adherence to routines, ritualized patterns of verbal or nonverbal behavior; excessive resistance to change. • Highly restricted, fixated interests. • Over- or under-reactivity to sensory input or unusual interest in sensory aspects of environment.	• Repeating the same words or sounds over and over; lining up toys; using self-stimulatory behaviors. • Insisting on specific responses to specific prompts; getting notably upset in the face of changes in plans, rules, roles, or expectations; insistence on sameness. • Inability to shift focus from specific topic of perseverative area of interest; strong attachment to unlikely objects. • Fascination with lights or spinning objects; aversion to certain sounds or textures; indifference to pain or temperature.
3. Symptoms must be present in early childhood.	Atypical restrictive, repetitive patterns of behavior relative to same-age peers; must be noted in early childhood. In some cases, social communication challenges may not become apparent until later in childhood.	In early childhood, lack of interest or engagement in unfamiliar activities; preferring to play alone; minimal eye contact; restricted play, e.g., lining up or dropping toys repeatedly; failure to respond to own name; possible loss of previously attained skills. In children, lack of interest in social connection, e.g. not seeking approval, not tuning in to surroundings; atypical use of pragmatic language.

continued

Figure 1.1: Practical Summary of Autism Diagnosis (*continued*)

Criteria	Common Components	Examples of What to Look For
4. Symptoms together limit and impair everyday functioning.	Social and behavioral idiosyncrasies consistently interfere with the student's ability to meet the expectable demands of home and school.	Symptoms are present across contexts: symptoms significantly interfere with the smooth functioning of daily life at home (e.g., meals, bedtime, sibling relationships) *and* at school (e.g., engagement in curriculum, socialization, transitions).
5. Symptoms are not better accounted for by an intellectual or other global developmental delay.	Autism spectrum disorder is a broad and pervasive diagnosis and cannot be diagnosed if less pervasive diagnoses are able to address all manifest symptoms.	Areas of differential diagnosis include social (pragmatic) communication disorder, social anxiety disorder, selective mutism, auditory processing or language challenges, attention deficit disorder, attention deficit–hyperactivity disorder, obsessive-compulsive disorder, Tourette syndrome, and many others.

Additional Considerations:

- An autism spectrum disorder diagnosis must be accompanied by a stated level of severity as follows: Level 1 ("requiring support"), Level 2 ("requiring substantial support"), or Level 3 ("requiring very substantial support"). The determination of level is dependent on the extent to which symptoms interfere with daily functioning.
- Autism can occur *with or without* intellectual impairment, language impairment, or other neurodevelopmental or behavior disorders. So, a student may have, for example, ASD with ADHD, ASD with OCD, or ASD with dyslexia. Or a student with ASD may be "twice-exceptional," meaning, in this case, that they have both ASD and superior intelligence or exceptional talents or skills.

Source: American Psychiatric Association, 2013. *Author's Note:* This table is for informational—not diagnostic—purposes. Autism can be diagnosed only by a licensed medical doctor (e.g. child psychiatrist, developmental pediatrician, or pediatric neurologist) or a PhD child psychologist or neuropsychologist, using resources and tools created specifically for the purpose of diagnosis. This process is often done in conjunction with a team that includes social workers and speech, occupational, and physical therapists, along with input from parents or guardians and school professionals.

Because the ASD diagnosis no longer uses subtypes to distinguish the many significant differences among individuals on the spectrum, diagnosticians must now elaborate on the severity of the symptoms. Doctors must specify whether the condition occurs with or without intellectual impairment; language impairment; a known medical or genetic condition or environmental factor; another neurodevelopmental, mental, or behavioral disorder; or catatonia. Along the same lines, diagnosticians now must also rate the social and behavioral symptoms as specifically as possible in order to characterize individuals and their degree of need, from Level 1 (requiring support) to Level 3 (requiring very substantial support) (APA, 2013).

The rest of this book explores these criteria in functional, school-related, "real-kid" terms. Even though all students diagnosed or classified with ASD meet the criteria, they do so in an endless variety of ways. That means that every individual on the autism spectrum is exactly that: an *individual* on the autism spectrum. Every such student will be uniquely different from every other—as different from one another as typically developing students are.

Setting an Inclusive Tone: What's in a Word?

The converse of *normal* is *abnormal,* a term that implies a less-than or even sinister status. You won't see either of those words in this book. Instead, this book uses the neutral, judgment-free terms *atypical and typical,* respectively, to refer to students who do and don't have special needs.

Taking the notion of typicality one step further, the term *neurotypical* was coined by some members of the autism community, in the 1990s, to describe people who are *not* on the autism spectrum.

From that notion of neurotypicality sprang a broader movement toward *neurodiversity,* which seeks to portray all natural variations in neurological functioning as benign and inclusive, implying that all neurological functioning lies on a spectrum. In this sense, every one of us, different as we are, has a place on the same universal, neurodiverse spectrum.

ASD at School

There are several common aspects of behavioral, social, and communication challenges that most students on the autism spectrum manifest, albeit in their own ways. Among your students on the autism spectrum, you can expect to see many who are preoccupied with specific activities and interests and highly dependent on routines and consistency. They may display repetitive and stereotyped motor mannerisms and extreme responses to sensory input. Most of these students make minimal eye contact, have difficulty with peer relationships and interactions, and show a lack of desire for socially or emotionally shared experience. Their expressive and receptive language skills may be delayed, limited, or idiosyncratic, and some students on the spectrum may be nonverbal.

It's important to note that contained within these characteristics are some apparent contradictions. For example, social communication challenges can present in some students as a complete *absence* of spoken language and in others as an *onslaught* of relentless or repetitive social language—and any variation in between. Sensory challenges can include both extremely *heightened* sensory reactions and extremely *diminished* sensory reactions—sometimes even within the same student. All of these complex challenges are addressed in depth the upcoming chapters.

Meanwhile, tucked in and around the many pervasive challenges are some significant strengths that are often overlooked. It's crucial that everyone working with students on the spectrum look closely for subtle strengths and call them out whenever we can, so that neither we nor our students get discouraged by their many in-your-face challenges.

Call It Out: Detail Detection

One of the greatest learning challenges students on the autism spectrum face is understanding the big picture—that is, really getting the gestalt of a lesson or concept. Indeed, students on the spectrum are often so mired in the veins on the leaves that they miss the entire forest—and the trees, too! (Read about supporting big-picture learning in Chapter 6.) In certain contexts, however, there can be tremendous value to their degree of attention to detail. Many students on the autism spectrum have powerful memories and keen perceptions of numerical patterns, inconsistencies, and items out of place. They can be quite expert at tasks requiring repetition or precision, such as data entry, problem solving, and pattern analysis.

By the same token, thanks to that attention to detail, many students on the spectrum develop an expertise in an area of interest to them. Perhaps because they are unimpeded by awareness of the bigger picture and unaware of pressure toward social conformity, they tend to dive deep into the weeds and often cultivate an extraordinary base of knowledge on a single topic. While that topic may be of questionable value to the curriculum, it is often nevertheless an impressive body of knowledge. (Learn more about singular focus in Chapter 2 and about how to add curricular value to those interests in Chapter 6.)

Call It Out: Rule Reliance

Students on the autism spectrum are eager cooperators and rule followers. Because rules add so much comprehensible structure to the day, these students may cling to school and classroom rules like the lifeline they, in fact, are. This means that as long as students on the spectrum understand the rules precisely, they are likely to be the most reliable rule followers and cooperators in the school. They may, in fact, take their rigid adherence to the rules a bit too far at times by policing their peers. Still, it's important to note that these students are doing what they are told. And that is a standout skill in the school setting.

Call It Out: Truth Telling

Students on the autism spectrum have difficulty taking the perspective of other people. While this often makes them unaware of how their words and behaviors may impinge on the comfort of others, it also makes them blissfully free of worrying about how others will perceive them. For this reason, students on the spectrum are unlikely to be manipulative; they don't connive to change the way others think because they don't tend to think about what others think! (Read more about perspective-taking in Chapter 5.) Likewise, these students don't generally perceive any reason to lie. When you stop a student in the hallway and ask why they are not in music class, they are unlikely to make up an excuse. In order to do so, they'd have to anticipate what you want to hear and what you don't want to hear, and then manipulate the situation to their benefit. Seeing no reason to be anything but honest, they respond, plainly, "The music teacher has bad breath."

Setting an Inclusive Tone: Inside/Outside

Perhaps the most confounding differences among students on the spectrum relate to whether the symptoms of their autism are primarily internal, primarily external, or a bit of both. Because the symptoms of ASD can vary so greatly from one student to another, it is easy to generalize and make assumptions about these students on the basis of what you see. Don't do it. It's a surefire way to underestimate or overestimate these complicated individuals.

For example, many students on the spectrum wear their challenges on their sleeves; their autistic symptoms are instantly apparent to others. These external challenges can include flapping hands, rocking back and forth, limited or nonstop verbalizations, idiosyncrasies of speech such as echolalia, and idiosyncrasies of language such as one-sided conversation or immersion in obscure topics. (Read more about the idiosyncrasies of communication in Chapter 5.) Students like these should not be considered "low functioning," even though their outward appearance demonstrates such obvious challenges. Don't underestimate them! These students who exhibit their symptoms externally may be cognitively and creatively strong or even brilliant; they may be experts in a narrow area of know-ledge or proficiency or even excellent all-around students.

Alternatively, some students on the spectrum struggle with challenges that are primarily internal. They may present rather typically at first, able to engage in wholly appropriate greeting rituals or brief encounters. They may be articulate, intelligent, and coherent in basic conversation; their bodies may be calm and composed. Students like these should not be considered "high functioning" even though they do not present external challenges. Don't overestimate them! Inside, their cognitive processes may be deeply disorganized, their receptive language severely limited, their minds profoundly preoccupied with rigidly restricted, repetitive topics. They need more support and patience than you might expect.

ASD: Getting the Big IDEA

Some students on the autism spectrum arrive at your school with a diagnosis in hand and a roadmap in place. They may have received many years of special education support and individualized services before coming to you. Other students may come to you having fled or been booted from a prior placement that wasn't a good fit. Others arrive with no diagnosis or classification at all.

Some of them may have managed to get by without special supports or special education in previous placements. Many students on the autism spectrum can pass under the special ed radar during the early elementary years because they are articulate and bright enough to function independently at school. Yet as they move through the elementary years, the curriculum begins to require abstraction and higher-level thinking, and socialization begins to demand spontaneity and reciprocity. So, in the mid- to late-elementary years, what was seen as "quirkiness" devolves into "dysfunction," and the academic and social gaps become too wide to overlook.

Whether the students you work with are already known to be on the spectrum, or your teachers are just beginning to suspect that they are, you can be sure they will need more support than do typical students. Fortunately, there are many federal, state, and district guidelines and systems that exist to help.

In 1997, the Individuals with Disabilities Education Act (IDEA; formerly the Education for All Handicapped Children Act) guaranteed students with disabilities a free and appropriate public education (FAPE) in the least restrictive environment (LRE). In 2004, the reauthorization of IDEA went further, requiring that schools provide children who have special needs with an education equal to that of their typically developing peers.

In 2017, the U.S. Department of Education amended IDEA to align it with the newly authorized Every Student Succeeds Act (ESSA; formerly No Child Left Behind). Today, that amended version of IDEA requires that states establish performance goals for students with disabilities that are aligned with the goals of their typical peers and report their progress on standardized tests. Further, the law contains provisions designed to increase graduation rates and decrease dropout rates.

As the ideals of IDEA have evolved over the years, their interpretation and application have evolved as well. As recently as 2017, in the case of *Endrew F. v. Douglas County School District,* the U.S. Supreme Court ruled in favor of a higher standard of education for students with special needs by clarifying the FAPE mandate. Whereas "free, appropriate public education" had previously been interpreted loosely enough to allow the education of these students to be only marginally appropriate, the word *appropriate* would now require schools to consider individual students' strengths and challenges and to write and follow an individualized education program (IEP) with objectives that are ambitious in light of individual students' circumstances (U.S. Department of Education, 2017).

These changes signaled clearly to the education world that it was time to start thinking outside the self-contained classroom. As a result, today, students on the autism spectrum, along with those who have other learning challenges, populate our mainstream schools and general education classrooms in record numbers. In fact, the most recent data show that 91 percent of students on the autism spectrum attend mainstream (i.e., not exclusively special ed) schools, with a plurality spending at least 80 percent of their school day in general education/inclusion classrooms (U.S. Department of Education, 2019). In response to this influx of students with special needs in general education settings, educators continue to cast around for education models that best serve all students—with and without special needs—and best serve their teachers, families, schools, districts, and communities. Welcome to the era of inclusion.

Leading the Way to Successful Inclusion

Public school options for students with special needs have evolved in both name and practice. What used to be *mainstream schools* are now *inclusive schools*. What used to be *self-contained classes* and *mainstream classes* have morphed into *special classes* and *inclusion classes,* respectively. What used to be *mainstreaming*—that is, students on the spectrum visiting a mainstream class occasionally—is now all about weaving these students into the fabric of a diverse class full-time, with plenty of support and differentiation. What used to be a system of exclusion is now a system of inclusion. And what used to be a clear-cut separation between general education and special education is now quite a bit more fluid.

A Measured Approach to Meeting Needs

The first approach teachers take to address the skill or performance challenges of students is RTI (response to intervention). Referenced in the 2004 reauthorization of IDEA, RTI directs teachers to collect data over time, intervene and adjust instruction as needed, and monitor responses—all according to a tiered system. Today,

RTI is generally subsumed within the broader system known as MTSS (multitiered systems of support). These tiered approaches are much more proactive and productive than the wait-to-fail approach (or, effectively, the wait-to-fail *response*) that preceded them.

RTI is a proactive, evidence-based approach to identifying and supporting struggling learners by closely measuring the progress of all students and providing targeted, leveled intervention. While RTI is not federally mandated, it is being implemented to some extent in at least 94 percent of school districts across the United States (Belisle, 2017).

Using RTI, general educators can conduct a Tier 1 universal screening to assess the skill levels of all students. Through this screening, some students will be identified as below grade level in reading or math. Those students will be provided with supplemental instruction during the school day in an effort to help them meet grade-level expectations.

Students who do not achieve adequate progress after approximately eight weeks of Tier 1 supplemental intervention are moved to Tier 2. This level of intervention includes more intensive and targeted support that is matched to individual need. Tier 2 support is usually provided in small-group settings that are supplemental to the general classroom setting.

If adequate progress is not demonstrated with Tier 2 supports after a full marking period, Tier 3 intervention may be indicated. Tier 3 interventions are more individualized, intensive, and comprehensive than those provided at Tiers 1 and 2. Students who do not demonstrate progress as the result of Tier 3 interventions are to be referred for an evaluation for special education eligibility, at which point data from Tier 1, 2, and 3 interventions are taken into consideration.

It is important to note that an active RTI process does not preclude parents or guardians from requesting and being granted a special education evaluation at any time during the RTI interventions.

The Special Education Evaluation

To initiate a special education evaluation, schools must have a written request or consent from a parent or guardian. Teachers or school counselors should explain the evaluation process to parents or guardians, framing the referral as a means of determining the best ways to support the child's success. Parents and guardians are often wary of special education evaluations for a variety of practical and emotional reasons. (See Chapter 8 to learn what that resistance is about and to collect strategies for guiding and supporting parents and guardians along the way.) Be sure to assure them that evaluations are conducted individually and confidentially and can be provided by the district at no cost to the family.

Special education evaluations usually include most or all of the following individual assessments.

Psychological evaluation. A psychologist assesses a student's intelligence (according to IQ testing), emotional functioning, and coping skills. The psychologist or other clinical professional may also meet with parents or guardians to assemble a social history—also known as a *psychosocial evaluation*—in order to collect information about birth and family history, developmental milestones, and living circumstances, as well as prior schooling, interventions, therapies, and any other salient events in the student's life.

Educational evaluation. An educational evaluator looks at academic achievement in terms of broad and specific math and reading skills. These skills are scaled according to age- and grade-equivalency norms.

Physical and occupational therapy evaluations. A physical therapist assesses gross motor skills (e.g., climbing stairs, jumping, running). An occupational therapist assesses fine motor skills (e.g., gripping a pencil, cutting with scissors, manipulating small objects) and sensory integration, which is the way sensory input is received in the brain. In many cases, a student's overall academic or behavioral functioning may be significantly compromised by matters of coordination or sensory integration. (Learn more about motor issues and sensory integration in Chapter 4.)

Speech-language evaluation. A speech-language therapist or pathologist evaluates a student's ability to receive and express information via the use of speech and language. Challenges in this area can include forming letter sounds, word retrieval, auditory processing, and social language. Even students who are quite articulate can have significant delays or distortions in their processing and use of language. Conversely, students who have very limited speech may in fact have strong language comprehension skills that might easily be overlooked. Students on the autism spectrum in particular may have excellent speech skills but struggle with the pragmatic or interactive aspects of language. Challenges in any of these areas can indicate the need for speech and language support. (See more on communication in Chapter 5.)

Decisions About Service Provision

When all evaluations have been completed, a meeting of the multidisciplinary or special education evaluation team is convened to synthesize all results. In this way, a complete picture of a student's functioning is painted in terms of strengths, challenges, and needs, and a plan of action is formulated. Generally, these meetings include a classroom teacher, the student's parents or guardians, all contributing evaluators, a representative special education teacher, a psychologist, the committee chair, and sometimes other relevant professionals or members of the community.

The goal of the evaluative process is to ensure that every student has access to a free, appropriate public education. If the process determines that a student's current education program is not appropriate to meet their needs, program placement must be changed, or modifications and accommodations must be enacted in accordance with the regulations laid out in IDEA. As a result of this process, an assortment of the following mandates may be enacted.

Mandated Plan Options: 504s and IEPs

Students who are found to have a discrete physical or cognitive challenge that directly impedes their ability to function at school (e.g., challenges related to walking, breathing, seeing, hearing, speaking, writing, reading) may qualify for a Section 504 accommodation plan under the Americans with Disabilities Act (ADA).

The ADA, which is a civil rights statute, protects individuals from impairment-based discrimination. A 504 plan is individually crafted by the team according to ADA regulations and grants students certain accommodations, such as preferential seating, large-print text, a ramp into the school building, and assistive technology to allow them equal access to education. With the playing field essentially leveled in these ways, these students would be expected to be able to reap the full benefit of their education program.

An individualized education program (IEP), on the other hand, is reserved for students who need more than a leveled playing field; they need an *adapted* playing field. Preferential seating or large-print texts would not be enough to give these students equal access to education. Instead, the evaluation team may determine that a student requires special education supports and services, as specified by the IDEA, in order for them to learn and function in the education setting. All provisions that might have been granted in a 504 plan can be included under the broader reach of an IEP. Given the pervasive symptomatology of ASD, most students on the autism spectrum qualify for an IEP.

In an IEP, the team can mandate a type of classroom or school program and a student/teacher ratio, the frequencies and student/teacher ratios of related services, and specific program accommodations and modifications (as described below). The team also establishes short-term benchmarks and long-term goals for every aspect of a student's program. The IEP becomes a blueprint for the student's learning environment and must be followed closely and updated every year. It is the responsibility of the student's teachers and other team members to uphold the mandates of the IEP and to monitor progress toward the IEP goals. The IEP requires educators to

- Actively pursue the acquisition of academic, social, and behavioral benchmarks with an eye toward long-term goal achievement.
- Oversee the implementation of accommodations and modifications.
- Keep careful data regarding progress and concerns.
- Stay alert to specific conditions or circumstances that affect the student's ability to function.
- Facilitate collaboration and continuity among all members of the team, including the family.
- Report on the student's progress at multidisciplinary team meetings.

Accommodations and Modifications

Members of the multidisciplinary or special education team also recommend specific accommodations and modifications for students who have 504 plans and IEPs. Most districts use computer programs that generate 504 and IEP templates and offer menus from which to select appropriate accommodations, modifications, and relevant academic goals. All of these options are considered and discussed by the team before they are approved and entered into the official document.

Accommodations are changes made to a student's program to enable equal *access* to instruction or assessments. Accommodations do not alter the curriculum; they serve only to reduce the effect a disability has on the student's capacity to access education. Accommodations can be granted in various areas, including the following:

- *Presentation of information.* Accommodations in this area include "talking textbooks," "directions read and clarified," and "class notes provided."
- *Provision of response.* Accommodations in this area include allowing students to dictate and record answers for assessments and access to spell check, a calculator, and other assistive technology.
- *Setting.* Accommodations in this area include "preferential seating," "separate location for testing," and use of sensory tools to support functioning.
- *Timing and scheduling.* Accommodations in this area include extra time to complete work, periodic breaks during work activities, and the opportunity to complete assessments across several days.

Whereas accommodations affect *how* a student learns, modifications affect *what* a student learns. Modifications are changes made to the curriculum itself in order to meet the needs of the student. Common modifications include teaching only select aspects of the curriculum, reducing the amount of class work or homework, and assigning alternate questions or projects.

Education Settings and Supports for Students on the Spectrum

Federal law dictates that school districts must provide services to students with disabilities in the least restrictive environment (LRE) based on individual needs. This means that students with IEPs must, *to the greatest extent possible,* be granted access to mainstream programming, assessments, learning opportunities, and activities alongside typical students. For every student, the team must consider all placement options, beginning with the least restrictive. When an appropriate placement recommendation is agreed upon, a rationale for the rejection of less restrictive placements must be provided on the IEP.

Education placement options for students on the spectrum range from least restrictive (e.g., the general education classroom) to most restrictive (e.g., homebound instruction or residential facility). In between lies a wide variety of options mandated on the basis of a student's specific strengths and challenges. Note that individual states or districts may have different options or use different names and acronyms for the programs described here.

The General Education Classroom

A standard general education classroom is a conventional-size class run by one credentialed general education teacher. This is considered the least restrictive environment for all students. A small percentage of students on the spectrum are able to manage in a general education classroom with only minimal support, such as accommodations, modifications, and related services to help them stay afloat.

Related Services

Most students on the spectrum qualify for pull-out or push-in related services in conjunction with their program. These individually mandated services may include occupational therapy, speech-language therapy, physical therapy, counseling, consultant teacher support, resource room instruction, and reading support. Related services can be provided in conjunction with any classroom or program placement.

The Inclusion Classroom

The inclusion classroom model places students who have special education needs together with typical students in a conventional-size class, with the significant addition of built-in special education support. This model often allows students to remain with their typical peers all day, while incorporating a differentiated approach to mainstream curriculum and providing additional classroom support as needed.

Depending on the needs of students, inclusion support can range from classrooms that are co-taught by general and special educators, to the occasional push-in or pull-out support of various special education staff, to a classroom paraprofessional or aide assigned specifically to a student who needs one-to-one support. The most robust version of an inclusion classroom is one that features the full-time collaboration of a credentialed special education teacher right alongside the general education teacher.

Inclusive programs offer the distinct advantage of providing students with special education support in the context of the general population. Many students on the spectrum benefit academically, socially, and emotionally from this model. But it's not for everyone. There are students on the spectrum who simply cannot function in an environment as stimulating and rigorous as an inclusion classroom. (Read more about inclusion classrooms in Chapter 8.)

Special and Self-Contained Classrooms

A *special class* is a small, exclusively special education class with a student/teacher/assistant ratio of 12:1:2 or even 6:1:2, depending on needs and mandates. Such classes offer more specialized instruction and protection from the mainstream than inclusion classes do, but less access to the social modeling of typical peers. In secondary grades, students in special classes navigate the building independently and may be placed in any combination of special classes and inclusive or general education classes on a per-subject basis.

Similar to a special class, a *self-contained class* is a small, exclusively special education class with a small student/teacher/assistant ratio. But a self-contained class usually provides highly specialized and individualized instruction and an alternate curriculum, and it may follow an autism-related or other specific academic and behavioral protocol, such as TEAACH or applied behavior analysis (ABA). At the secondary level, students who are placed in a self-contained class tend to remain in one classroom and with a single group of classmates for the majority of the day.

Even when students spend most or all of their day in more restrictive classrooms like these, their presence in an inclusive school means that they should still be included in all schoolwide activities and events to the greatest extent possible. Modifications and accommodations may need to be made in order to enable these students to be able to participate, but schoolwide and districtwide activities should be formulated in a way that is specifically welcoming and comfortably accessible to all.

Out-of-District Placements and Non-Public Settings

Some small public school districts that have relatively few students needing special education services establish a system of reciprocity with neighboring districts. In these arrangements, special education services, resources, and funding are shared and available to students in both districts.

However, if a district's evaluation team determines that the district does not have the ability or capacity to provide the kind of programming a student needs, it may recommend a non-public placement: a privately run, publicly funded special education program. Because all students in this type of program have special education needs, interaction with typical peers is not available. Therefore, non-public placement is considered to be more restrictive than any of those listed above. Non-public placements can be fully self-contained day schools, residential schools, or hospital- or clinic-based day treatment centers.

Parents and guardians who are dissatisfied with a public school placement may request a non-public school or other more restrictive placement for their child. When the district affirms that it cannot meet a student's needs, it bears the responsibility of paying for the non-public placement. For this reason, many districts are reluctant to stipulate that they cannot meet the student's needs in-district. It's a conflict of interest often perceived by parents and guardians as denying their child the right to a FAPE. This can lead to bitter disputes between families and school districts and may result in legal action.

One-to-One Support

To bolster success in any of the settings mentioned, some students may be mandated to receive the support of a full- or part-time, one-to-one paraprofessional or aide. An aide's role is to provide individual academic, social, and behavioral support. Aides may be appointed to support students on the spectrum in their efforts to engage, attend, communicate, transition, socialize, and modulate their reactions. An aide can be added to any classroom setting; however, the addition of an aide is considered to make any environment more restrictive.

Most Restrictive Environments

When a student's needs are not being met in any of the above environments, school districts are expected to fund placement in a highly restrictive setting. Students who need an immersive, self-contained environment can receive academic, emotional, social, and behavioral remediation in a therapeutic boarding school. Students who need clinical support in order to be safe and successful at school or at home may qualify for placement at a residential treatment center where they receive education along with intensive clinical intervention and 24-hour supervision. Students who are in crisis may qualify for temporary homebound instruction or in-patient psychiatric hospitalization.

Additional Interventions

Some students on the spectrum receive therapeutic programming from an early age. These intensive interventions, provided by public early-intervention programs or private organizations, seek to address global autism spectrum symptoms such as engagement, flexibility, regulation, and socialization. Each of these programs features a different approach, and most show demonstrated benefits that have inspired passionate supporters and advocates among therapists, teachers, and parents.

Applied Behavior Analysis

The most commonly used behavior approach for students on the autism spectrum is applied behavior analysis (ABA), which applies learning theory and scientific insights into how behavior changes in response to environment. Desirable behaviors are identified, taught, and encouraged through positive reinforcement, while undesirable behaviors are not reinforced or are gently discouraged. ABA therapists maintain careful, ongoing observation, measurement, and data collection to assess progress.

Discrete-Trial Training

A teaching strategy integral to ABA, discrete-trial training supports the acquisition of new skills by breaking down targeted skills and behaviors into achievable components. Many additional interventive models have spun off from the fundamental approaches first established by ABA.

DIR/Floortime

The DIR (developmental, individual-differences, and relationship-based)/Floortime model developed by Stanley Greenspan involves therapists and caregivers joining in activities of the child's choosing and influencing actions and reactions based on the individual child's developmental levels. The DIR/Floortime approach generates rich opportunities for guiding and redirecting relationship development, potentially influencing a child's social and emotional functioning.

Complementary and Alternative Approaches

Many parents or guardians of children on the spectrum work with psychiatrists or developmental pediatricians to use medication to treat some of the symptoms of autism. Others explore complementary or alternative treatments outside the school environment. There is a dizzying array of options available, and new approaches are being touted every day. Families may pursue alternative protocols such as special diets, nutritional supplements, chiropractic treatment, osteopathy, acupuncture, vision therapy, biofeedback, neurofeedback, and many others, all in an effort to leave no stone unturned in their quest to help their child.

These therapies may be time-consuming and very expensive, and in many cases the evidence of benefit is anecdotal rather than clinically or scientifically proven. Some treatments, like chelation or hyperbaric therapy, may pose health risks. With others, like meditation and massage, there's nothing to lose and often much to be gained. Although some of these interventions may seem dubious to you, try to keep in mind that many professionals, parents, and guardians believe strongly in their effectiveness. As professionals ourselves, we must be careful to accommodate and support these efforts in our inclusive and differentiated programs, while also promoting research- and evidence-based practices.

● ▲ ◆ ◀ ■

Now that we've explored the autism landscape and the general framework of supports, it's time to go deeper into the picture. Let's start with the ever-present challenge that lurks just beneath the surface: anxiety.

Anxiety

First, can we agree that we all feel anxious sometimes? How about *worried? Nervous? Unsure?* No? Are you *sure?* It's all the same, really—a feeling of uneasiness about an imminent event, an unknown outcome, an unclear expectation. A bit of anxiety is a natural feeling, a healthy feeling. Without it, we might be dangerously impetuous or reckless or arrogant. But it's a fine balance: too much anxiety, and we become immobilized or frantic or overwhelmed.

Students who are on the autism spectrum face such a pervasive array of challenges that anxiety is always hovering, poised to disrupt their equilibrium.

Decoding Anxiety

As an education leader, you have learned, perhaps with the occasional exception, to believe in yourself and in your ability to meet your own and others' expectations. When confronted with situations that push you out of your comfort zone, you have most likely developed cognitive-behavioral ways of coping with your anxiety. You probably use cognitive strategies like accessing prior knowledge, predicting logical outcomes, placing your worries in context. Maybe you use behavioral strategies like practice, self-talk, sticky note affirmations. These are all coping skills; they are fluid and adaptable and, therefore, fairly reliable. Should they fail you, you can flexibly and often subconsciously revise them, try something else, and get back on track. Those skills have helped you get to where you are today.

Most students on the spectrum have had far fewer successful experiences on which to base their sense of self. The universe provides them with a steady stream of negative feedback, which takes a toll on developing egos and can cause students to feel worthless and hopeless—two feelings that are neither healthy nor productive.

In fact, individuals on the spectrum are at least four times more likely to experience clinical depression in their lifetimes than are members of the general population (Hudson, Hall, & Harkness, 2019).

It is with good reason that these students doubt their ability to cope in new and varied situations. It is with good reason that they expect to be overwhelmed, over-stimulated, ostracized, and outcast; those experiences occur on a regular basis. And so, throughout their formative years, their sense of self takes a beating. Anxiety gets baked in.

Anxiety Triggers

In students on the spectrum, anxiety can be triggered at every turn. And a school day takes many turns. On any typical day in an inclusion classroom, new lessons, topics, and projects—each with its own set of rules and expectations—come at them every few minutes. Bodies move in unpredictable directions; conversations veer off on inscrutable tangents; teachers and students come and go; peace and chaos ebb and flow. On some days, there are assemblies, field trips, absent teachers and service providers, fire drills, lockout and lockdown drills. The cafeteria runs out of pizza. A classmate vomits. Even activities thoughtfully designed to engage and excite students—those one-minute dance parties, quick writes, turn-and-talks, group projects, or trips to the makerspace—can be incapacitating for students on the spectrum unless carefully presented in advance and, if necessary, adapted.

When unexpected events like these confront students on the spectrum, that heightened anxiety may shatter their fragile equilibrium. They may experience sensory overload. Flexibility and rationality may desert them. Self-regulation may cede control to impulses, and reactions can be wildly unpredictable. Communication skills may shut down, leaving most students on the spectrum unable to alert others to their mounting distress, and so sometimes their only means of expressing anxiety is through behavior.

For example, in his memoir *Look Me in the Eye* (2007), John Elder Robison, an adult on the spectrum, recalls playing with blocks as a young child:

> I never mixed my food, and I never mixed my blocks. Blue blocks went with blue blocks, and red blocks with red ones. But Doug would lean over and put a red block on top of the blue ones. Couldn't he see how wrong that was?! After

I had whacked him, I sat back down and played. Correctly. Sometimes when I got frustrated with Doug, my mother would walk over and yell at me. I don't think she ever saw the terrible things *he* did. She just saw me whack him. (p. 7)

In the situation described, Robison vents his anxiety and frustration the only way he can: through behavior. However, as is the case in most such situations, his behavior does not clearly or effectively communicate anxiety or the trigger for it. Who could have guessed that mixing the colors of blocks would kick off such a reaction? Well, as educators, we need to guess. In fact, to serve our students well, we need to *know*. We need to know what their triggers are and take preemptive action to keep those triggers from being pulled.

Equilibrium in students on the spectrum is precarious—easily upset and very difficult to restore. Worse yet, a loss of control can set off a chain reaction of chaotic events. Because they are upset, students on the spectrum may unwittingly violate their own precious external or internal rules. The class schedule may be delayed and items they depend upon may be misplaced or damaged. In this way, small upsets can easily snowball into major disruptions.

Not only do educators need to know about our students' specific anxiety triggers, but we also need to learn how to decode behavioral reactions to understand what drives them. One of the most valuable strategies for working with students on the spectrum is to look past a behavior to find out what triggered it, what's fueling it, and what it is communicating. We will explore ways to find the function of disruptive behaviors in more detail in Chapter 7, but for now, let's look at some of the common anxiety triggers students on the spectrum face. Sometimes the trigger is a sensory assault, sometimes it's a social affront, and sometimes it's a violation of internal or external rules or expectations. But almost always, anxiety is in the mix.

Something New

A new school year. One of the most overwhelming new situations students on the spectrum face is a new school year. Everything they grew comfortable with last year is now upended. There are new rooms, new faces, new routines, new rules, and new expectations—all at once. Learned behaviors performed diligently by rote last year may not fit the bill anymore. Breaking a rule is not an acceptable option for our rigid rule followers, yet the new rules may not be crystal clear at first—a paralyzing predicament. Anxiety builds.

Unfamiliar activities. Most experiences come with their own sets of implicit expectations. Neurotypical students tend to greet new experiences as adventures and opportunities for growth, even though they may feel twinges of anxiety. But new experiences stretch students on the spectrum beyond the critical safety of learned behaviors and far outside their meticulously guarded comfort zones. New experiences can be confusing and destabilizing. For example, neurotypical students may file into the marbled lobby of the county courthouse on a field trip and spontaneously modulate the volume of their voices in deference to the solemnity of the space. But students on the spectrum are unlikely to perceive such tacit differences or to recognize their implications. Suddenly they are being shushed and scolded—and they have no idea when the rules changed or why. Anxiety builds.

Something Unexpected

Deviations from the schedule. Most students on the spectrum function best when they know exactly what is coming up, exactly what's expected of them, and exactly how they are supposed to respond. When the twists and turns of the day are not clearly presented and closely adhered to, they have no idea what's going to come at them next or how to cope with it. Anxiety builds.

Alterations in the physical space. Familiar places can be sanctuaries for students on the spectrum. When these students walk into a classroom and find that the seats have been rearranged, a teacher's desk has been moved to the back, the interactive whiteboard is broken, the clock is off by an hour, or, potentially worst of all, a teacher is absent, their whole equilibrium may be thrown off. Anxiety builds.

Something Different

Transitional moments. Transitional moments are the small slices of time *in between* structured activities in a school day. They are fleeting and may seem insignificant, but to students on the spectrum, these moments of disorganization can be triggering. Everyone is working quietly, and all is right in the world, and then suddenly, the bell rings and the room erupts into chattering voices, clattering equipment, slamming books, scraping chairs, and moving bodies. All of the rules of the previous moment are suddenly and inexplicably irrelevant. Students on the spectrum are catapulted into a hallway jam-packed with the social, sensory, and spatial chaos that is *other students*. At times like these, all bets are off in terms of status quo and rote behaviors.

Even within a classroom, transitions require students not only to complete what they were doing before, which can be difficult, but also to shift gears physically and mentally to whatever comes next. Many transitions also require modulations of mood and behavior, such as shifting from loud, lively, and energetic to quiet, organized, and still—and vice versa. This expected modulation presents yet another challenge for students on the spectrum, who have trouble regulating their moods. (Read about regulation in Chapter 3.) Suddenly, nothing is as it was the moment before. Anxiety builds.

Separation. Parting from parents and guardians in the morning may be especially difficult for students on the spectrum. Given their multifaceted anxiety and difficulty coping with change, many students will struggle with saying goodbye to everything that is home and family as they move into a different environment. This can make the bus ride and school arrival particularly anxious times. (See the Appendix for tips to help bus staff understand and support these students during their time together.) Separation from certain important people, such as specific teachers or aides, or separation from certain comfort anchors at various times during the day can also compromise a student's status quo. Anxiety builds.

Comfort Anchors

Neurotypical individuals are able to navigate the twists and turns of a day by flipping through an array of coping skills before determining how best to proceed. Without even realizing we are doing it, we read the room, we read the feelings of the people around us, we recognize and interpret context clues, and we decode the hidden curriculum. (All of these are social skills, explained in Chapter 5.) We stop and think, we access learned behaviors, we read between the lines, and we get ourselves in gear. (All of these are executive function skills, discussed in Chapter 3.) Empowered by this robust skill set, we believe in our ability to cope with whatever comes our way.

Because students on the spectrum lack the flexible thinking capacity required to devise fluid and effective coping skills, they do their best to make the world around them feel as predictable and safe as possible by relying on a rigid set of rules, rote skills, objects, and events. In fact, most students on the spectrum would prefer that life be as it is in the movie *Groundhog Day*—that is, every day exactly the same as the day before.

That way, they would be able to use learned, rote behaviors over and over and always meet with the same result.

This need for sameness usually manifests as an insistence on repetitive conversation, a cognitive immersion in static topics, and an urgent need to organize certain aspects of their environment. Those reliable exchanges, rules, topics, and structures become anchors that help these students feel grounded as everything else swirls around them. For this reason, they often become experts in obscure, very narrow areas of personal interest, such as comic book heroes or batteries. They lock into fixed expectations, such as always taking the same exact route to school. They create rules for life, such as always wearing blue socks on Tuesdays—white socks are strictly for Fridays. They depend on your cheerfully perfunctory "Welcome to a brand-new day!" greeting being delivered *verbatim* every morning; if it's not, they may be on shaky footing for the rest of the day. These students order their world and adhere rigidly to that order in a quest for sameness, structure, and consistency. (Learn more about cognitive immersion in certain topics, aka *perseveration,* in Chapter 6.)

These kinds of touchpoints become *comfort anchors*—predictable moorings that students on the spectrum cling to in order to stay afloat. As long as life adheres to their internal rules and expectations, and as long as interactions never deviate, then the world feels safe and anxiety diminishes.

But of course, school does not lend itself to such a rigid structure, such a fixed mindset. An inclusion classroom demands flexibility and open-mindedness as well as engagement in the ever-changing landscapes of socialization, communication, information processing, and sensory regulation—each of which is a threat to a student's insular status quo. And so, anxiety can indeed be triggered at every turn.

Leading the Way to Successful Inclusion

The best way to help reduce anxiety at school for students on the spectrum is to make the school day and the classroom environment as predictable and consistent as is reasonably possible. This does not mean that general education teachers need to turn their classrooms upside down for the sake of a few students. But it is reasonable to expect teachers to provide the adaptations necessary to make the classroom a safe and welcoming space for all students—students on the spectrum included. Let's look at some ways this can be done.

Visual Schedules

Many effective tools can be mined from special education practices and modified for practicality and ease of use in inclusion classrooms. One such tool is the *visual schedule,* which is indispensable when working with students who are on the autism spectrum.

Visual schedules lay out the routine of the day for students in a way they will be sure to understand. By incorporating images in conjunction with or in place of words, visual schedules provide students with a reliable way of knowing what to expect. Although not all students on the spectrum need a visual schedule, it is a powerfully effective tool for those who demonstrate anxiety or problematic behaviors. When used consistently and mindfully, the schedule itself becomes a comfort anchor and, often, a linchpin of success in any classroom that serves students on the spectrum.

Young students and others who cannot read may benefit most from a visual schedule that displays photographic icons or simple line drawings of expected activities (see Figure 2.1). These icons, called Picture-Communication Symbols and commonly known as PC symbols—and are designed to facilitate comprehension and communication for students on the spectrum. The tens of thousands of PC symbols available to educators and families can be used interchangeably to represent upcoming activities on a schedule. PC symbols can also facilitate the exchange of ideas, thoughts, and feelings between students and teachers.

Visual schedules are highly comprehensible for students on the spectrum not only because the drawings or photographs on the cards are fairly concrete, but also because the manipulation of the cards themselves provides visual and tactile sensory input. When a task or activity is completed, the student pulls the representative icon off the schedule and

Figure 2.1: Visual Schedule

Source: SchKIDules, LLC. Reprinted with permission.

moves it to a "completed" column. For students who need an even more concrete type of representation, actual objects—like a plastic spoon to signify lunchtime or a ruler to signify math—can be affixed to a schedule. Both the schedule and the icons may be laminated and attached to each other with Velcro, or they may be magnetic.

Some students benefit from having the day broken down into even smaller and more manageable components. Subschedules, like the one in Figure 2.2, are a good way to present sequential and other discrete tasks.

Figure 2.2: First/Then Visual Subschedule

Source: SchKIDules, LLC. Reprinted with permission.

Students who can read or are somewhat less concrete in their thinking can use printed schedules composed of only words or digital schedules that can be manipulated onscreen. Although the tactile element of a printed schedule is critical for some students, the digital element of a computer schedule can be more fun and engaging, and more discreet for students who are tuned in to the social scrutiny of their peers.

Maintaining a PC Library

Picture-based communication symbols are available at teacher supply stores, from education catalogs, or through apps and software programs. Once a teacher has collected a cache of standard PC symbols, the icons can be used and reused for years. The investment of extra time and energy on the part of the teacher to promote effective communication in this way will be recouped many times over by the powerfully enhanced capacities and diminished anxiety that have been facilitated for the students.

Be mindful that the cost of compiling a comprehensive array of PC symbols may be prohibitive for many teachers. To support your teachers who are working with students on the spectrum, ensure that your school or district invests in a complete set of downloadable PC symbols that can be shared by educators and used extensively for years to come. (See the Resources section at http://barbaraborson.com for links to teacher-focused training materials, PC symbols, and icon libraries.)

Teachers can create visual schedules for the class as a whole, providing an organizing and clarifying resource for all students. But it may be especially effective to individualize a schedule for students on the spectrum and for others who need support with organization and transitions. Individualized schedules can be displayed on or in a student's desk, on a wall adjacent to the desk, inside a folder, inside a classroom cubby, or on the outside or inside cover of a binder.

Respecting the Schedule

Visual schedules can allow students on the spectrum to set aside some of their anxiety, relax some of their rigidity, and cope better with the inevitable fluidity of the day. But schedules are effective only if students can rely on teachers to follow them unwaveringly.

The responsibility of adhering religiously to the schedule may cause teachers to become a bit tenacious about maintaining the plans and expectations of their day or even their week. The reality of educating students on the autism spectrum means that teachers must, by necessity, abide by their schedule with a greater degree of intensity than they otherwise would. Be mindful of which teachers have students whose day will be irrevocably derailed by an unexpected change in plans. As a rule of thumb, handle these classes with care; contents are very fragile. Whenever possible, alert these teachers well in advance if you plan to fiddle with their regular daily schedule. Let them know beforehand when you will be coming into the classroom for an observation or just for a visit—even if advance notice is not usually your style. Alert them if you will be shaking up the recess schedule "just for variety." Tip these teachers off before any fire drill, lockout drill, or lockdown drill so they can prepare specific students who need help getting through these kinds of unscheduled events.

Building Transition into the Schedule

Brief as they are, transitions demand scheduling, too. Encourage teachers to provide students with specific transition schedules that detail not only what comes before the transition and what comes after, but also what is expected of them *during* the transition. Figure 2.3, on page 39, provides an example of a visual transition schedule with images.

Setting an Inclusive Tone: Continuity and Collaboration

To optimize students' functioning throughout the day, schedules need to be applied consistently across contexts. All members of the inclusive school community should be aware that change is a challenge for every student on the autism spectrum, so they all need to be part of the effort to preempt difficulties for these students. Visual schedules can and should be implemented by everyone in the building who works with students on the spectrum, including therapeutic providers, special area teachers (e.g., arts, physical education, music), nurses, cafeteria workers, recess monitors, secretaries, custodians, and bus staff.

To facilitate this collaborative environment, ensure that all school faculty and staff have access to as much practical information as possible about students on the spectrum—both in general and in terms of specific red flags regarding specific students. (See the Appendix for reproducible Fact & Tip sheets, customized for all members of the school community.) Try to implement these inclusive practices:

- Invite ancillary faculty and staff to team meetings, prioritizing their availability when scheduling.
- Support the sharing of resources and specific strategies to include special area teachers, therapists, and building staff and bus staff within the bounds of confidentiality.
- Encourage classroom teachers to share icons (or access to icons) with everyone who works with their students; to prepare transition schedules for students to carry from one location to another, as needed; and to help special area teachers and therapeutic providers create specific schedules for their time with these students.

Figure 2.3: Transition Schedule

Leaving Science

1. When your science teacher tells you to clean up, stop working.

2. Hang your goggles on a hook.

3. Gently place equipment that you used into the lab sink.

4. Wash your hands and then dry them with a paper towel.

5. Discard the paper towel into the wastebasket.

6. Line up quietly.

Students should be encouraged to carry their transition schedules from one activity to the next. Not only does a transition schedule provide coherence to an otherwise incoherent interval, but it also serves as a transitional object—a portable comfort anchor—weaving a tangible thread of continuity from one activity or environment to the next.

Teacher Absences

Teachers represent a crucial comfort anchor for students on the autism spectrum. Especially in classrooms that have only one teacher, nothing at school proceeds reliably when that teacher is absent. Not only does a substitute teacher look and sound and smell different from the usual teacher, but the all-important schedule may be violated or even overlooked entirely.

When assigning substitute teachers, try to prioritize your classes with students on the spectrum. Do you have substitute teachers in your cache who are familiar with ASD? If you don't, then plan to include your usual subs in autism-related professional development trainings. Having established, knowledgeable, go-to substitute teachers for your classrooms that serve students on the spectrum means that these students will be greeted with some degree of familiarity and informed continuity, which can dramatically improve the outcome of an otherwise high-anxiety day.

Drilling Down into Emergency Drills

Emergency drills can be disconcerting and scary for typical students; they can be overwhelming and deeply distressing to students on the spectrum, whose baseline anxiety levels are already heightened.

It's good practice for every teacher of students on the spectrum to prepare topical mini-schedules at the beginning of the year and carry them at all times, tucked inside an attendance book or anything else that is reliably brought along during a drill. These schedules should outline the anticipated proceedings of a drill and demonstrate exactly what students are expected to do. For example, a mini-fire drill schedule might show icons that depict "Quiet mouths," "Get in line," "Follow the teacher," "Quiet hands and feet," "Wait for instructions," and so on. Once students have acclimated to using a mini-schedule during drills, the schedule itself can serve as yet another comfort anchor as well as a behavioral guide during any actual emergency. Expectations for drills can also be supported through the use of social stories, which are described in detail in Chapter 5.

Contingency Planning

Even with the consistent and continuous use of visual schedules, it's still (to some extent) anyone's guess what will actually happen next in an inclusion classroom that has many bodies in motion at all times. There are some circumstances that *no one* can predict. At any given moment, a classmate gets a bloody nose. The classroom sink overflows. The gerbil escapes its cage. Because unexpected events can be so distressing to students on the spectrum, it's vital that teachers have contingency plans to help them through these situations, which can escalate quickly on multiple fronts.

When something unexpected occurs in the classroom—like the gushing nose, the overzealous sink, or the rogue gerbil—students on the spectrum may react intensely, not only to the drama of the emergency itself but also to the fact that it was unscheduled. Encourage teachers to carry a PC symbol at all times that conveys a clarifying or reassuring message like "Pause for an emergency interruption!" or "Hold onto this card until I'm available to give you my attention again. I'll come back to you as soon as I can!"

Take measures to ensure that every teacher of students on the spectrum has another teacher on standby in case of classroom emergencies. Co-teachers, parapro-fessionals, or teaching assistants can plan to divide and conquer. If there are no other adults assigned to the classroom, encourage teachers to buddy up so that a neighboring teacher is prepared to step in for urgent backup support until the nurse, custodian, counselor, or other helper can arrive.

● ▲ ◆ ◀ ■

Helping students on the spectrum manage their anxiety is crucial. An excess of anxiety can derail not only an individual student's own functioning but also the homeostasis of the whole class. Reactions of students on the spectrum come out in big ways. In the next chapter, we will look at why reactions can be so intense and unpredictable and at what you can do to help.

Executive Function

Underlying the many challenges described in this book is one that compounds the rest. Executive function is a neurologically based set of self-regulating skills that enables us to get things done. Difficulties with executive function can cause students to struggle with such critical skills as making plans and decisions, staying organized and focused, managing impulses and emotions, and learning from mistakes. In a broader sense, difficulties with executive function are believed to inhibit social understanding and social interaction and contribute to restricted and repetitive patterns of behavior, reactivity, and other hallmark traits of autism spectrum disorder (Demetriou et al., 2018).

While disruptions of executive function are believed to be associated with atypical functional connectivity between regions of the brain, scientific theories differ on whether the issues relate to underconnectivity, overconnectivity, or a variability of connectivity among regions (Maximo, Cadena, & Kana, 2014).

Regardless of its etiology, executive function is the challenge that makes the other challenges more challenging. Difficulties with executive function cause students on the autism spectrum—and some other students, too—to be unable to cope effectively with their other challenges or with the situations that trigger them. This means that when they react, they react in big ways. And so, even as we adapt the environment to reduce the triggers, we also need to look at ways to teach and support coping skills.

Decoding Executive Function

Do you ever stop to appreciate the inner workings of your personal computer? Aside from periodically updating them, we generally take computer operating systems for granted—until they get glitchy or break down. And then, suddenly, we are hobbled, helpless, hopeless. It's so frustrating. We are so dependent on our computers to do what we want them to do that we are utterly incapacitated when they don't perform as expected.

A computer operating system supervises the functioning of all the computer's applications, scripts, programs, and all other related and interconnected systems. It's what enables a computer to execute a user's commands. It regulates input and output; it filters out junk and other extraneous data; and it organizes files, providing a framework for sharing and receiving information.

The human brain comes hardwired with its own operating system that supervises the functioning of all the body's interconnected sensory, regulatory, and behavioral systems. Our executive function system manages the execution of our brain's commands, regulates input and output, filters out junk and other extraneous data, and organizes our mental files, providing a framework for sharing and receiving information. Take a look at Figure 3.1 for a snapshot of the many ways in which a computer operating system parallels the brain's executive function system.

Figure 3.1: Computer Versus Human Operating Systems

Function	Computer Operating System	Human Operating System
Command execution	Executes users' commands to perform various operations, such as saving files, running programs, and printing.	Executes cognitive commands to perform various actions such as activating prior knowledge, persisting on tasks, and following instructions.
Information oversight	Oversees input and output of information, such as data, correspondence, documents, reports, presentations.	Oversees input and output of information and reactions, such as cognitive organization, metacognition, decision making, impulses.
Resource management	Maintains system resources, such as memory, file storage, processing time, and disk space, allocating and prioritizing them as needed.	Maintains cognitive resources, such as memory, processing time, pacing, prediction, reflection, attention, flexibility, and following directions, allocating and prioritizing them as needed.
Network facilitation	Facilitates file sharing and networking functions.	Facilitates the flow of social interactions and communication, ensuring a smooth exchange of information.

As you'll see, when their executive function systems fail, students are left hobbled, helpless, and hopeless, and likely to fail, too.

Brakeless Behavior

When their executive function systems are compromised, it's difficult for students to stop and think before they act. They can go too far in any one direction: laughing too hard or for too long, getting too wild or too silly. They may be unable to shift gears from active to still or from loud to quiet—and vice versa. They may be unable to stop whatever they're doing, unable to adapt their behavior based on circumstance or context, or unable to generalize from experience. Neurologist Martin Kutscher (2004) calls this *brakeless behavior*.

In the classroom, executive dysfunction has an impact on almost everything our students are expected to do academically, behaviorally, and socially (see Figure 3.2).

Executive Function at Work

Executive function is the brain's ability to think through situations and, when necessary, override impulses or automatic reactions. For those of us with adequate executive function skills, the frontal and prefrontal lobes in our brains operate as the chief executive officer, directing every choice we make and everything we do. Executive function effectively orchestrates and regulates our actions and reactions in the context of conscious consideration and learned behavior. So it's executive function that reminds you to take a deep breath before walking into a Board of Education meeting and to bite your tongue as the meeting proceeds; it's what gets you back to work the morning after the budget was voted down. Executive function is our micromanager and our cognitive interface, the crucial filter between impulses and actions.

But executive function can be a challenge for many kids, and it can affect every aspect of their functioning. The absence of crucial executive function skills can cause students to appear inconsiderate, rude, impulsive, rigid, careless, stubborn, inattentive, highly reactive, thoughtless, impatient, disorganized, or disoriented. Executive dysfunction is to blame for many of the barriers to learning for students who are on the autism spectrum as well as for students who have attention deficit hyperactivity disorder, fetal alcohol syndrome, learning disabilities, mood disorders, obsessive compulsive disorder, and traumatic brain injury.

Consider how these challenges might play out in a typical school scenario. Let's say that near the end of a school day there is an assembly that will continue until dismissal. Teachers are advised to dismiss their students directly from the auditorium after the assembly rather than have them stop back at their classrooms first. What effects might this seemingly small deviation from routine have on Samir, a student with executive function challenges? Keep an eye out for expected skills, listed in Figure 3.2, as we muddle through this experience with Samir.

Even on a regular day, *navigating the transition* of leaving school to head home is an arduous task. As explained in Chapter 2, *shifting gears* from the relative comfort of school to the unstructured and minimally supervised bus ride is a major daily hurdle. The challenge involves not only the transitional stress triggered by getting

Figure 3.2: Challenges of Executive Dysfunction

Area of Impact	Executive Function Skills	
Academics	accessing working memory activating prior knowledge contextualizing information focusing on tasks following instructions generalizing information	making inferences reading between the lines regulating pace starting, pausing, and stopping work updating information using metacognition
Behavior and coping	adapting to change adjusting mood being patient considering context controlling impulses learning from mistakes	modulating reactions persisting with tasks shifting gears staying calm thinking flexibly tolerating frustration
Self-determination and socialization	expressing empathy keeping track of belongings making and keeping friends managing time and space navigating transitions organizing work	planning actions and reactions predicting outcomes reflecting on antecedents sharing with peers taking turns thinking objectively

to, boarding, and settling into the relatively chaotic environment of the bus; it's also that the entire bus ride itself is one long transition—a bridge between school and home. So, dismissal, under the best circumstances, is a double whammy: it's a transition to a transition. This is why, at dismissal, Samir clings particularly tightly to his familiar routines. The insertion of an assembly at this relatively tumultuous time of day adds even more stress because it is a break from and a violation of those anchoring routines. Even if his teachers put icons on his schedule in advance to forecast the assembly and the auditorium dismissal, it's all a deviation from the norm, a transition heaped on top of other transitions. Samir's anxiety is ratcheting up and his coping skills are slipping away.

But that's not all. Loss of access to the classroom before leaving the building for the day means that students have to pack up earlier than usual and tote their backpacks to the assembly—which in turn requires *predicting outcomes, planning actions and reactions, organizing work,* and *keeping track of belongings.*

Attending the assembly requires skills like *shifting gears, processing information, managing time and space,* and *focusing on tasks,* herculean efforts that are further compromised by the common sensory challenges of an assembly such as crowds, amplified announcements and music, and applause. (Read more about sensory challenges in Chapter 4.)

At the end of the assembly, students may be dismissed by class rather than by bus, which is another deviation from the norm; this requires *thinking flexibly* and *following instructions.* The route through the corridors from the auditorium to the buses is entirely different from the route from the classroom to the buses. This means Samir has to forgo important comfort anchors like his requisite daily high five with the assistant principal on his way to the exit.

The class might leave the building through a different door than usual, and therefore, once outside, Samir's spatial understanding and perspective on the array of buses in the driveway may be completely askew and require *updating information, generalizing information,* and *thinking more flexibly.* (Read about visual and spatial challenges in Chapter 4.)

As these stressors layer atop one another, coping skills like *tolerating frustration, staying calm, considering the needs of others,* and *controlling impulses* become so elusive that anxiety can boil up into dysfunctional behavior. Now Samir is refusing to get on his bus, insisting that it's in the wrong position and therefore must not be his bus, even though its number, its driver, and the color of its sign are all unchanged. And now Samir is crumpled on the sidewalk, eyes squeezed shut, rocking hard forward and back, and desperately invoking the comfort of the familiar by yelling insistently, "May the Force be with you! May the Force be with you!"

None of this is to say that assemblies are necessarily nonstarters for Samir or any other student on the spectrum, or even that having assemblies at the end of the day is a bad idea. Not at all. Instead, let this scenario serve to point out just how fragile the equilibrium of these students is, how compromised their functioning can be by something even as seemingly innocuous as an assembly, and how much consideration must be paid to easing their way.

Leading the Way to Successful Inclusion

To someone who doesn't know better, a student who is melting down on the sidewalk by the buses while conjuring Obi-Wan Kenobi might be judged as noncompliant, oppositional, irrational, and nonsensical. This assessment could lead to swift disciplinary intervention, which would be neither appropriate nor helpful in this case. In fact, it would make the situation even worse. On the other hand, being aware of the role that executive dysfunction plays in crises like this allows school leaders, teachers, and building and bus staff to implement effective interventive measures and—better yet—preventive measures. Let's look at options for both.

Debriefing and Relearning

After a negative experience or incident, once all is calm and equanimity is restored, it's imperative that the debriefing process elicit a cognitive awareness about what happened, what didn't go so well, and what could be done differently to ensure a better outcome. Although most of us use executive function skills on a conscious or subconscious level, those skills are often derailed by impulses for students on the spectrum. It's virtually impossible to interrupt or divert the impulse train once it's rolling, so the most effective teachable moments with these students will happen later, during peaceful, nonthreatening times when new strategies can be learned and perhaps assimilated into a kind of muscle memory.

Setting an Inclusive Tone: Access Empathy

It is important to remember that when students on the spectrum break the rules, they are rarely grandstanding or being oppositional. It's much more likely that the reason they are off task is that they have not adequately understood or effectively generalized the rules, or that they do not have the necessary executive function skills to meet expectations. (Read more about challenges to generalization in Chapter 6.)

It follows, then, that disciplinary interventions are counterproductive in response to behaviors that result from executive dysfunction. Consequences and other punitive measures serve only to further elevate anxiety and eclipse coping skills, and they usually fail to teach the necessary new skills. Access your own impressive executive function capacity by meeting challenging behaviors with patience and understanding, even as you support skill building. In this way you are modelling coping skills for your struggling students and setting a tone of empathy and acceptance for your faculty, staff, and student body.

Ideally, students would jump eagerly on board to collect new ways of approaching situations. But realistically, the relearning process is a difficult one, and the motivation to try may be minimal. As we all know, making changes to our own ways of functioning requires metacognitive skills like reflecting, predicting, planning, persisting, focusing, thinking flexibly, learning from our mistakes, updating information . . . the very skills we are seeking to teach! Helping students learn the skills they need to help them learn is a Sisyphean task, but it's one that can be achieved with lots of repetition and patience.

Here is a three-step process you and your teachers can use to debrief a challenging experience and transform it into a teachable moment.

Step 1: Encourage reflection. In order to help students become conscious about what's going wrong, we need to guide them to reflect on past experiences. Most of us subconsciously and automatically reflect on our past experiences—both failed and successful ones—and we adapt our behavior accordingly to optimize success going forward. Students on the autism spectrum, however, are not likely to embark on this journey of growth without guidance, nor are they likely to learn spontaneously from their past experiences.

Reflection is the first part of facilitated debriefing. To be effective, a reflective process must define and explain fundamental interactive building blocks like cause and effect, action and reaction. We need to guide students to reflect on both unsuccessful and successful experiences, helping them to work backward to discover how a particular outcome was generated by a cause and how certain reactions resulted from certain actions. Samir might not be able to be articulate or indicate what led him to sink to the sidewalk outside the school. In his case, it was a series of events. But taking the time to revisit the experience with him when he is calm, and to consider and review how the situation escalated, can give us clues as to what his triggers were.

Reflection also involves considering past scenarios from multiple perspectives. Adopting the perspective of others is another process that is not likely to happen spontaneously due to a challenge called *mindblindness* (discussed in Chapter 5). Role-play is a powerful way for students on the spectrum to experience the effect their actions might have or have had on other people. Have these students re-enact their own role in a situation, but also have them take a turn enacting other people's positions. This enables them to understand the experiences of others in a more concrete way.

Step 2: Guide prediction and practice. Even though, with our help, students on the spectrum may be able to reflect on what went well or not so well in a prior experience, don't assume that this epiphany will guide them to make changes to their future behavior. They may not intuit that continuing to enact that same behavior will yield the same undesirable results every time. We need to teach them that, too.

Guide these students to use the information they have gathered from reflecting to help inform a guess or prediction about what will happen if they approach a problem or situation the same way again. This step may seem painfully obvious to you, but it needs to be made overt for students on the spectrum: If they want a different outcome, they need to change their approach, their input. Conversely, if they don't change their input, they will not obtain a different or better outcome.

Help students to visualize themselves in the same or a similar situation again. Encourage them to consider different ways of responding to or preparing for the challenges. Then, have them practice or role-play different ways of acting in the situation, including both the ways they acted and reacted before as well as new, alternative approaches. Guide them to imagine and practice enacting various possible outcomes. Ask Samir questions like, *How about we come up with a way to make sure you have all your stuff before you go to an afternoon assembly?* Or, *What are some other ways you can recognize your bus besides its location in the line?* Or, *Let's figure out some other ways you can let us know you're upset.*

Step 3: Facilitate a plan. Help students make a specific plan for how they will implement their new skills in a variety of situations. Help Samir to make dismissal checklists or transition sub-schedules. Help him create a social story that outlines what he should expect and how he should behave before, during, and after an assembly. Have him draw a picture of his bus that includes all of its identifying signifiers to carry with him at dismissal. Appoint a buddy to accompany him to the bus and identify the meeting place where they will link up. (Learn about social stories and buddy systems in Chapter 5.)

Samir might also be willing to broker a deal through which he gets a double high five from the assistant principal in the morning if he missed his dismissal high five the day before. That would build some helpful flexibility into his routine.

Also be aware that the responsibility of learning from situations like these should not fall only to the student. Take the opportunity of debriefing to examine what could have been handled better on the classroom and school level. What triggers could have been predicted and preempted? What signs of escalation were overlooked? What interventions could have happened before Samir hit the pavement? (Read about decoding behavior and responses in Chapter 7.)

But even after some cognitive awareness is instilled and some specific new plans are put in place, our students will continue to meet with failure if their executive function skills lag behind the social, academic, and behavioral expectations in the classroom. This means teachers must also focus on skill building.

Skill Building in the Classroom

In co-taught inclusion classrooms, one of the teachers can take certain students aside in a small group to adapt assignments or lay out upcoming events for those who need skill-building support for executive function. That teacher can review and break down expectations, checking for understanding. She can teach students to chunk assignments into smaller tasks to help students feel gratified and energized by mini-accomplishments, so they won't have to sustain their attention and effort toward achieving a more elusive goal. She can show students how to pace themselves, how to use strategies that promote persistence and frustration tolerance, and how to pause to make predictions and plans. She can provide graphic organizers and teach students how to approach tasks in a structured and organized way. Even as these students get started on their differentiated activities or projects, the co-teacher should touch base with them frequently to guide them to reflect on their progress, update information, review facts to boost their working memory, make inferences about the project to put it into conceptual context, and draw connections between their work and their learning goals.

Along with the use of supportive tools, it's also important to provide students with natural opportunities to strengthen and flex their executive function muscles throughout the day. Here are some strategies teachers can use to help build those muscles.

A Process for Processing

Teachers can remind students to wait, plan, reflect, stop-and-think, and so on, by incorporating relevant icons at opportune places on the schedule so that students are prompted to practice those skills regularly. This helps make the processing routine conscious for particularly impulsive students and for anyone else who might otherwise blow right past it.

Parallel Process

In a well-differentiated inclusion classroom, executive function supports do not take much time for teachers to implement. But they do require forethought. One might even say they require some solid executive function skills on the part of teachers. Teachers need to stop and think to predict what specific circumstances are likely to trigger individual students, use creative and flexible thinking to differentiate interventions for specific students, plan ahead to optimize outcomes, set goals and follow through on their achievement, and be able to stick with the plans until the new skills are assimilated. Try to be supportive and patient with your teachers as they try to be supportive and patient with their students.

Strategies for Sitting Tight

Waiting means deferring gratification, which is especially difficult for impulsive students who have limited executive function. Worse, when students on the spectrum are told to wait, they often do nothing but that. There is no notion of finding something else to amuse themselves in the meantime or occupying themselves while they wait. Instead, they just wait, and they perseverate on what they are not getting. And that makes waiting interminable.

Teachers can provide tools and strategies to help these students sit tight. Often creating a protocol—or mini-schedule—called "Things to Do While Waiting" can be helpful. Practical options include fiddling with a small fidget toy, crossing one's fingers, counting breaths, and silent singing.

Prompts for Emotional Awareness

Teachers can provide students with a visual tool that helps them tune in to their escalating levels of stress. An emotions thermometer can be taped to the desk of younger students or accessed digitally by older students (see Figure 3.3). Students can point to a level on the thermometer or name the associated color to indicate where they are at emotionally and where they may be headed. This provides teachers with an opportunity to intervene before behaviors escalate. Teachers might respond by taking a student aside to help her communicate her distress. They might provide a sensory break to help a student let out pent-up energy, frustration, or overload. (Read about sensory breaks in Chapter 4.) They might call for a counselor.

Another helpful approach is for teachers and individual students to work collaboratively to determine specific preemptive strategies that are likely to be most helpful as things are heating up, as well as which strategies are best avoided. While many students on the spectrum may not be able to provide this kind of insight themselves, you can bet that their parents and guardians know what helps and what makes things worse. Information is power; it's our responsibility as educators to find out all we can. (Read more about parent and guardian perspectives and find a useful tool for tapping their wisdom in Chapter 8.)

Figure 3.3: Emotions Thermometer

Note: A free reproducible emotions thermometer is available for download from http://barbaraboroson.com/Emotions-Thermometer.pdf

● ▲ ◆ ◀ ■

Understanding that the reactions of students on the spectrum are at the mercy of executive function is a crucial component of effective leadership. Just as important, however, is developing an understanding of the wide assortment of sensory triggers that can set off those poorly controlled reactions. Unfortunately, it's a perfect storm. Hang on tight: we're heading straight into it.

Sensation

The baseline, hypervigilant state of students on the autism spectrum has been referred to as "defense mode" (Raede, 2018). As discussed in Chapter 2, their anxiety systems are always on high alert, braced against unpredictable input. One of the most intense and unpredictable assaults against their equilibrium comes at them in the form of sensation.

Decoding Sensation

As many as 95 percent of students who are diagnosed with autism spectrum disorder (ASD) have some degree of sensory processing disruption (Tomchek & Dunn, 2018). Challenges can occur in any or all of the three components of the sensory system: sensory modulation, sensory discrimination, and sensory-motor integration.

Sensory Modulation

Sensory modulation refers to the way sensory input is received and processed in the body. A useful way to understand sensory modulation is to imagine that every individual comes preset with a sensory dial. Most of us sport functional sensory dials that are calibrated to allow just the right amount of sensory input into our systems most of the time. But the sensory dials of students on the autism spectrum are not calibrated quite as effectively, sometimes letting in too much sensory input and sometimes too little. Moreover, those dials are loosely anchored—they slip easily out of position. In practical terms, this results in an extremely capricious sensory system that can lead to dramatic compensatory behaviors.

Sensory avoidance. When the sensory dial is wide open, too much sensory input can flood the system, causing students to experience sensory overload. They may be overwhelmed by an unfettered onslaught of input: the grating sound of chair legs scraping against the classroom floor, the glaring light of the document camera, the caustic smell of shellac in the art room, the sour taste of the orange juice in the cafeteria, or the nubby texture of the rug in your office. In response, they may seek to avoid or protect themselves from the impact of that excess sensation by pulling their hoods up over their heads, crawling under their desks, or even running away. Most likely you've seen these students covering their ears and crying as they exit the school when the fire alarm is ringing—or even the dismissal bell.

Sensory seeking. On the other hand, sometimes students' sensory dials can be too tightly closed, not allowing enough nourishing sensory input into their systems, causing a kind of sensory deprivation. When this happens, students may feel lethargic, and, as a result, will seek out additional sensory input any way they can. They may rock back and forth, tip their chairs back, hum to themselves, get up frequently out of their seats, stand too close to others, pace the room, chew on their collars, and so on.

Sensory Discrimination

Another sensory challenge that affects students on the spectrum is *sensory discrimination,* which is the ability to distinguish and understand changes in the sensory environment. As is the case with sensory modulation challenges, sensory discrimination challenges can take very different and opposite forms.

Sensory detection. Sometimes students on the spectrum can detect very subtle discrepancies in their sensory environment and therefore may perceive details most of us overlook. They may be the only ones in art class who can recognize the difference between royal blue and cobalt; they may hear nuanced elements of music that can't be heard by the average listener; they may be the first to notice that the school food service has changed chicken nugget suppliers. They may also be the first to smell smoke or gas.

Sensory jumbling. Other times, students on the spectrum really struggle to differentiate variations in their sensory environment. They may not be able to discern the difference between rhyming and non-rhyming words or distinguish visually between foreground and background information. They may not perceive that they have food on their face or recognize when they are getting too hot or too cold. They also may be unable to discern the difference between a friendly tap on the shoulder and an aggressive poke or smack on the arm—a confusion that has significant social implications.

Sensory-Motor Integration

The third challenging aspect of the sensory system is *sensory-motor integration,* which is the ability to both plan and execute motor responses to various situations or stimuli. Sensory-motor integration involves three little-known and inconspicuous senses and their interaction with a skill called motor planning.

- *Interoception.* The interoceptive sense is our awareness of our own internal states, such as balance and position as well as hunger, thirst, fatigue, illness, and other types of physical discomfort. Students who are not getting enough interoceptive input may not notice that they are quite sick, feverish, or off balance, and they may miss the signal when it is time to use the bathroom. On the other hand, students who are overwhelmed by internal input may seem hypochondriacal, but, in fact, they are feeling every internal irregularity quite acutely. A paper cut may be truly painful.

- *Proprioception.* The proprioceptive sense helps us gauge where our body is in space based on the input or pressure we receive through our joints and muscles. Proprioception gives us information about what our body parts are feeling or doing or *should* be doing in any situation. Students who seek proprioceptive input may chew their pens, crack their knuckles, or play a little too rough. Conversely, students who are overwhelmed by too much proprioceptive input may avoid being touched or be unable to wear tight-fitting clothes or tolerate chewy or crunchy foods.

- *Vestibulation.* The vestibular sense tells us—literally—which end is up, based on the position of our heads in relation to the earth. Students who crave vestibular input tend to be risk takers: They may enjoy spinning, climbing, and endlessly swinging. They may test the interplay between balance and gravity by habitually tipping their chair back so that it hovers on its back legs. Conversely, students who are overwhelmed by vestibular input tend to feel physically unstable: they may get dizzy easily, avoid high places, and cling tightly to the banister on stairs.

- *Motor planning.* Difficulties with motor planning, sometimes known as "dyspraxia," can include crossing the midline (i.e., performing tasks that require the eyes or hands to work across the front of the body, such as reading all the way across a page, drawing a circle, or tying shoes) and organizing body movements. Dyspraxia can make it difficult for students to execute visual-spatial tasks that require bilateral coordination or multistep motor activities like getting dressed, typing, using a computer mouse, taking notes, throwing a ball, playing piano, riding a bike, or swimming.

Sensory Safety: A Cautionary Tale

Students with challenges to any of the three internal senses must be closely supervised at all times because their health, balance, and stability—and, critically, their *perception* of their health, balance, and stability—may be dangerously impaired. This means that some may take significant physical risks with no awareness of the peril, such as jumping down whole flights of stairs or hanging from unstable places. Others may be quite unwell or injured and not realize it, or they may not be stable enough to safely participate in physical activities independently.

When my son was 6 years old, my husband showed him how to use a small zipline contraption at a playground. Back and forth our son zipped, his hands wrapped around the handle above his head, while my husband walked alongside, supporting him at the hips. Eventually my husband asked our son whether he was ready to go it alone, and our son responded affirmatively. My husband said, "OK, I'm letting go now," and my son immediately fell the three feet to the ground and broke his arm.

Despite all the practicing, my son's proprioceptive system had failed to transmit the message to his brain that he'd have to bear his own weight now, and therefore his brain had failed to signal his hands to actively grip the handle over his head. So when my husband let go, there was nothing and no one holding my son up—not even himself.

The Clash of Sensory and Motor Planning Skills

When challenges related to the internal senses and to motor planning intersect, students struggle with *sensory-motor integration*. They may exhibit weak muscle tone and body control: slumping in their chairs, sprawling on the rug, appearing generally floppy and clumsy. They tend to have difficulty figuring out how to approach certain visual-spatial and sensory-motor tasks, such as how to hold a piece of paper still with one hand while erasing on it with the other or how to coordinate the opposing movements of their arms and legs to execute jumping jacks. They may stomp their feet or walk on their toes, smack too hard when giving a high five, or press so hard with their pencil that they tear the paper they're writing on. They may avoid running or jumping activities, fail to hold on tight to a handle or exert adequate pressure on a lever, or be unable to adjust the position of their body for momentum while swinging on a swing set.

Self-Stimulation (Stims)

Because their systems are so capricious, some students on the spectrum seek to regulate for themselves how much sensory input they receive. Beyond sensory-seeking and sensory avoidance efforts, they may use idiosyncratic behaviors to either activate or soothe their sensory systems. These kinds of behaviors are *self-stimulatory behaviors,* commonly known as "stims." Stims include flapping hands, rocking, twirling, blinking, flicking fingers, repetitive nonverbal vocalizations, pacing, and even head banging, scratching, and biting. Although stims are not used consciously or deliberately by students, it's necessary to be aware that they do serve important functions.

Stims can serve to energize sluggish students, helping them stay alert and engaged. This is why you may see some students vigorously chewing on their hair or their collar while doing schoolwork, tapping their foot while reading, or rocking back and forth while listening.

Paradoxically, students who are feeling overwhelmed or overstimulated may use stims to help them calm down. It may be hard to imagine that adding more sensory stimulation could help students feel less overstimulated. But, in fact, stims can help these students to tune out an overwhelming sensation by focusing their attention on an action that is familiar and of their own making. For them, tuning in to the smooth rhythm of rocking may help them tune out the chaos all around them. Stims may also help students release excess energy or excitement, which also serves a soothing, calming function.

Predictable Unpredictability

Complicating the sensory picture is the fact that one student's response to sensory input may be quite changeable from sense to sense, from day to day, and even from minute to minute, making prevention and intervention particularly tricky. For example, Spencer may be soothed by a warm hug one day, but a hug or even a pat on the shoulder might overwhelm them the next day. Tina may flourish in the gym, despite the pounding of basketballs and the shrieks of skidding sneakers, but a single boom on the bass drum in orchestra might send her scrambling under the piano. Or Tina may have managed the noise in the gym just fine yesterday but be unable to tolerate it today because something else is compromising her ability to tolerate noise.

Leading the Way to Successful Inclusion

Not only are students on the autism spectrum easily triggered by sensory stress, but because of executive dysfunction (as discussed in Chapter 3), their reactions to that stress may be unpredictable, impulsive, and poorly regulated. For students, for teachers, and for you, this presents a real challenge.

Identifying effective preemptive strategies and interventions for students on the spectrum requires a bit of detective work, along with some trial and error. Even more than typical students, students on the spectrum benefit from behavior analysis that helps shed light on the antecedents or triggers of problematic behaviors. Because students on the spectrum have so many potential trigger areas—and often a wide assortment of communication challenges as well—behavior analysis can yield quite revelatory results. (More on this topic in Chapter 7.)

Understandably, many educators (and parents, too) are eager to curtail reactive behaviors like stimming. Some stimming behaviors may interfere with learning. Others, like head banging, may cause harm. And sometimes adults seek to stop stims in the interest of helping a student appear more typical. Indeed, students who are flapping and making noises don't blend subtly into the background. But know this: *Stims are not negative behaviors* to be discouraged with token economies or other behavior management systems. *Stims are coping mechanisms.* And extinguishing coping mechanisms serves only to extinguish coping.

Remember that these reactive behaviors are symptoms of a deeper problem and a signal to educators that something is amiss, that the student's system is out of balance. In fact, for some students on the spectrum who have difficulty with speech and language, behavior may be their only means of communicating sensory or other distress. (Read more about communication in Chapter 5 and more about behavior *as* communication in Chapter 7.) In order to effect meaningful change, we must address the problem at the level of causation. That means investigating the environment to look for sensory and other triggers and then designing effective interventions by adapting the sensory environment and introducing replacement behaviors.

Adapt the Sensory Environment

Making adaptations to the sensory environment will go a long way toward relieving sensory stress and reducing the need for reactive behaviors.

At the classroom level, adapting the sensory environment can mean turning off some of the lights, modulating the noise level, reducing distractions, rethinking seating arrangements, and incorporating optional movement breaks into the day. Additionally, certain individualized adaptations may go a long way toward helping specific students. Here is a collection of ideas to consider.

Flexible Seating

Adapting the classroom sensory environment can mean moving a desk away from the open windows and the distracting activities outside or away from the classroom door and the noise of the hall. Don't be alarmed to see a student's desk facing away from the interactive whiteboard or somewhat separate from the rest of the class. Sometimes teachers find that providing a study carrel or test dividers or placing an empty or backward bookshelf alongside a student's desk can provide a buffer against unrelenting sensory input. It can be overwhelming for some students to manage a shared physical space, a shared social space, and a bustling sensory environment all while trying to engage in the curriculum.

Let teachers know that you understand and accept the need for unusual seating arrangements and other creative classroom adaptations, provided that such adaptations are facilitated in a way that does not make a student feel singled out or inadequate to a task.

Sensory Sanctuaries

A sensory sanctuary is a place that is available to students when they want or need to regroup. It is a welcoming, supervised area that invites students to self-soothe or vent excess energy. Sensory sanctuaries can be set up in various configurations.

Sensory corners. Best suited for elementary or self-contained classrooms, sensory corners can be defined by placing a small rug in a corner of the room partly blocked off by bookshelves or cabinets. In the sensory corner, teachers can set out an assortment of quiet, safe, and soothing sensory items: squeeze balls, Play-Doh, Slinkys, stress balls, pull tubes, kinetic sand, therapeutic putty, earbuds for listening to music, noise-canceling headphones, a beanbag chair or Yogibo, a rocking chair, stuffed animals, and so on. This becomes a cozy place that can be available for any student who needs to retreat and regroup now and then. For students on the spectrum, it can truly be a sanctuary.

Sensory rooms. In recent years, inclusive elementary and secondary schools have had great success converting a large hall closet or a small office into a friendly "sensory room." Larger and more comprehensive than a sensory corner, a sensory room can be lined with mats on the floor and the walls and set up to allow students to discharge gross motor energy via mini-trampolines, stationary bikes, balance balls, and even swings. In addition, sensory rooms can contain potentially calming elements such as textured or weighted balls, a soothing sound machine, lava lamps, sandboxes, weighted blankets, and so on. These spaces have become so popular that they've gone mainstream. Many inclusive schools make them available to any student who needs them, and they have shown therapeutic benefit for anyone who needs a break now and then.

Sensory paths. Another option is to create sensory paths in school hallways (see Figure 4.1). Many young students love being guided to play hopscotch, walk on tiptoe, and circumvent obstacles while simply moving from room to room or on an as-needed basis. By the time they arrive at their destination or return to the classroom, their senses are refreshed, and they are ready to learn.

Be aware that although sensory corners, rooms, and paths may become indispensable retreats for some students, they can be overwhelming for others. Use of any sensory sanctuary must be strictly voluntary and self-selected. Be sure that participation is never mandatory, never imposed or punitive, and never, ever confused with seclusion. (Read about seclusion in Chapter 7.)

Figure 4.1: Hallway Sensory Paths

Photos courtesy of Rachel P. Smith, Principal, Edgewood Elementary School, Whiteville City Schools, Whiteville, NC.

Maximizing Minimalism

In order for any student to be ready to learn, the classroom should feel safe and comforting, not chaotic and confusing. Highly decorated spaces can be overwhelming environments for students on the spectrum. Teachers working in inclusion classrooms around the country have shared with me that this creates a bind for them. They feel significant pressure from their administrators to create a highly decorated and visually stimulating classroom environment. They know that administrators are looking to see bright, cheerful bulletin boards, extensive displays of student work, posted classroom expectations, informative content graphics, and more. I've consulted in inclusion classrooms where even the ceilings and the windowpanes were covered with decorations and student work, where the teachers tell me, regretfully, "Our principal expects to see this!"

Let teachers know that you realize that in this era of inclusion, classrooms aren't necessarily what they used to be. Comfort means different things to different people. Let them know that you know that classrooms don't have to be chockfull of displays to appear friendly, cheerful, and welcoming. Assure teachers that you get it, that you understand the need for minimalist décor and other classroom adaptations for the sake of your inclusive student body. Help them to explain this new perspective to parents and guardians, too.

In fact, you can even bolster their efforts by offering teachers some minimalist tips.

Keep it clean and clear. Organized spaces are significantly less overwhelming than disorganized spaces because they are more easily comprehensible. Better yet, an organized external environment actually fuels an organized internal environment. With that in mind, encourage teachers to do the following:

- Create clear boundaries around classroom stations and center areas, and label specific areas with straightforward names.
- Clearly label equipment storage areas.
- Arrange displays on bulletin boards in neat, perpendicular segments that have blank space between them where the eyes can rest.

Let less be more when it comes to décor. Suggest that teachers cover some bulletin boards with bright, solid-colored paper—and nothing else. That creates attractive and cheerful décor that is neither distracting nor chaotic.

Let the SMART Board speak for itself. Advise against attaching decorations, charts, calendars, or other information directly to the surface or on the edges of interactive display screens. There is enough stimulation coming through the screen itself—movie clips, music, zooming satellite maps, pop-up animations, and numbers and sentences that appear and disappear. As engaging and interactive as this content may be, it can be a lot to take in. Leaving the edges of interactive display screens clear gives the eyes a break, draws focus toward the center, and visually separates foreground from background.

Making the Sensory-Sensitive Classroom Work for Everyone

Some inclusion teachers feel quite torn—even resentful—about having to "turn down the volume" on their classrooms. They might worry that accommodating a couple of students' needs means depriving the rest of the class of something engaging and rewarding. For example, at one school where I consulted, a teacher, Enrique, did not want to give up his routine of treating his students to "Funky Fridays"—playing dance music on Friday afternoons. But his students on the spectrum could not tolerate the noise.

Integrating students who have special needs into inclusive settings means that the mainstream environment must be adapted somewhat to accommodate their special functional and learning challenges. But you can assure your teachers that you do not expect them to upend the gestalt of their entire classroom for the sake of a few students. Creative, differentiated adaptations and accommodations are key.

Rather than abandon his weekly dance party, Enrique considered holding his weekly dance party during a time when his sensitive students would be out for resource room or therapy, even if that would mean transforming Funky Fridays into Techno Tuesdays. He also thought about providing noise-blocking headphones to his sensitive students during Friday's funk time. But in the end, the best solution was one that would allow everyone to participate: he turned Funky Fridays into a silent dance party, during which every student wears earbuds and dances with abandon to their own choice of music—or silence.

Introduce Replacement Behaviors

In addition to adapting the sensory environment, teachers can help individual students replace disruptive or dangerous sensory reactions with more adaptive behaviors that fulfill the same function.

If, for example, Charlie is continually poking his peers, behavioral consequences such as removing privileges or changing his seat assignment will not address his sensory need. In fact, instead of curtailing the problematic behavior, those kinds of quick-fix responses could cause the behavior to escalate because they fail to address the problem at the level of causation.

Alternatively, encourage teachers to be on the lookout for sensory reactions and to introduce replacement behaviors that serve the same function as those reactions but in more adaptive, less disruptive ways. When Charlie pokes his peers, he is most likely seeking proprioceptive input via his hands and fingers. Providing something suitable for him to poke that has a similar texture (but won't poke back!) could put an end to the provocative behaviors. A bit of putty, a squeeze ball, a Koosh ball, a squishy toy, a hacky sack, or even a soft pencil grip might be stashed in a desk or pocket for permissible poking anytime.

Also important to consider in this scenario is the possibility that Charlie is poking peers not for sensory reasons but in an effort to make social contact. Many students on the autism spectrum lack either the speech skills or the pragmatic language facility needed to initiate a conversation in an expectable way. If Charlie's teacher feels that the poking behavior is meant to serve a social function, then productive social skills and strategies can be taught to replace the off-putting poking. (Read about communication and social challenges in Chapter 5.)

Accepting a New "Normal"

Giving teachers the green light to implement replacement behaviors also means accepting the possibility of unconventional circumstances that go beyond alternative seating and decorating strategies. Let teachers know that you understand why you're seeing what you're seeing. Discuss with them the ways in which an inclusion classroom is expectably different from a conventional classroom and the ways in which the administration might support these changes. Let's look at some examples.

Keep on moving. Students who need movement or vestibular input may stand or pace during lessons, sit on therapy balls at their desks, or be given frequent opportunities to change position. Many schools have incorporated adaptive furniture into classrooms, enabling all students to learn in physical positions that are most effective for them. Adjustable-height "standing" desks allow students to sit or stand while working, as they choose. Pedal desks include foot pedals or swinging bars near the floor to keep restless feet quietly occupied.

Work it out. Students who need proprioceptive input may wear a weighted vest, weighted lap pad, or weighted shoulder pads. They may be given opportunities to engage in "heavy work"—weight-bearing activities, such as collecting books, pushing carts, holding doors open for the class, or carrying equipment bags to and from recess or PE. They may be encouraged to work off some energy and stimulate their muscles through a set of chair push-ups, planks, or jumping jacks before a period of quiet work.

Chew on this. Students who tend to bite or chew on inedible objects may benefit from frequent snacking on crunchy or chewy foods that provide oral or proprioceptive input, such as pretzels, granola, carrots, or dried fruit.

Change it up. Students who are overwhelmed by input may need to do modified or alternate versions of activities that may be triggering or too intense for them.

Affirm Occupational Therapy

Occupational therapists are a wonderful resource for suggestions about tools and equipment that would help adapt the sensory environment and replace disruptive sensory-seeking behaviors. Remember that occupational therapy (OT) is not just for addressing motor challenges; it's for sensory support, too. Occupational therapists can help teachers obtain bumpy cushions, pencil grips, vibrating pens, weighted vests, bean bag chairs, and much more. You can find links to resources like these at http://barbaraboroson.com.

Setting an Inclusive Tone: "Fair" Is Not "Equal"

Teachers may need to be granted special dispensations to adapt the sensory environment for students in ways that do not conform to general school rules. For example, wearing a baseball cap can help to relieve visual overstimulation and vestibular instability. Chewing gum provides oral and proprioceptive input and can also boost auditory processing and focus. Listening to music through earbuds can soothe students and enable them to tune out extraneous noise and focus on the task at hand. Be flexible enough to grant exceptions that are necessary to the effective functioning of your special students.

These may be indispensable modifications for students on the spectrum, but they may also be objectionable to their peers. Teachers in inclusion classrooms may hear a lot of "Hey, that's not fair!" when some students are allowed to chew gum or use their phones to listen to music while others aren't. No two students' needs are quite the same. If all students were treated equally—that is, exactly the same way—no one's needs would be well met. Differentiated education is about giving every student what he or she or they need. If Kareem objects when Fiona is allowed to wear a baseball cap in class, teachers can explain that wearing the baseball cap helps Fiona to be successful at school. They can assure Kareem that he'll get whatever he needs in order to be successful, too. That's the difference between equal and fair: Equal means everyone gets the same thing; fair means everyone gets what he or she or they need. Be sure you have your teachers' backs as they explain their actions to students and parents who may not understand the inherent individualization of the differentiated inclusion classroom.

Additionally, occupational therapists implement sensory interventions that can help regulate sensory systems on a deeper level. These may include joint compression and deep pressure (which help to regulate proprioceptive input), therapeutic swinging (which helps to regulate vestibular input), and therapeutic brushing (which helps to desensitize nerve endings by stimulating them incrementally). These kinds of activities support the organization of the sensory system to calm students down and set them up for learning.

● ▲ ◆ ◀ ■

Even after the day has been scheduled, executive function skills have been supported, the sensory environment has been adapted, and replacement behaviors have been encouraged, effective social interaction remains a significant obstacle to the success of students on the spectrum in inclusion classrooms. In the next chapter, we'll take a look at the myriad challenges students on the autism spectrum face in the area of socialization and communication and at ways to draw these students and their peers together.

Communication and Socialization

Typically developing children hone their social skills experientially. With every successful and every failed interaction, they subconsciously and spontaneously note which of their words are effective and which are ineffective, and which of their actions make other people happy or angry or sad. Then they adapt their developing behaviors accordingly. It's a kind of social osmosis that, over time, guides behavioral choices and manifests through personality. But that kind of social know-how does not develop organically among students who are on the autism spectrum, so their unexpected communications may result in confusing, difficult interactions, and their misguided social efforts often obstruct relationships. The absence of this all-important "social radar" is due to several specific challenges related to both communication and socialization.

Decoding Communication and Socialization

A student's facility with communication and socialization can be compromised by difficulties in several areas. *Speech and language* may be limited by issues with articulation and processing; *communication* may be compromised by issues with semantics and pragmatics; and *socialization* may be impeded by interactive obstacles like joint attention and mindblindness. These issues combine to make effective interaction one of the greatest challenges for students on the spectrum.

Speech and Language

Many students experience speech and language challenges at some points in their development. These common challenges may occur with or without autism spectrum disorder.

Speech challenges. Speech is the way we say words and sounds. Most speech challenges relate to the way we form and pronounce words, and they are often due to one of two causes:

- *Dyspraxia.* A problem with motor planning, dyspraxia (also known as "apraxia") causes students to be unable to navigate the process of getting words that are in their brains to come out through their mouths.
- *Dysarthria.* A neuromuscular impairment, dysarthria refers to a lack of muscle control that causes students to be physiologically unable to make their mouths form the words that are clear in their heads.

As many as 30 percent of school-aged children on the autism spectrum are thought to be minimally verbal or nonverbal. However, this information cannot be taken as an indication of their intelligence, their capacity to comprehend speech and language, or their ability to learn in a differentiated inclusion classroom (Tager-Flusberg & Kasari, 2013).

Language challenges. Language is the way we use words to communicate. Like speech challenges, language processing challenges can affect any student, including those on the spectrum. Common issues in this area include challenges of receptive language (understanding what others are saying) and expressive language (putting thoughts and ideas into words), as well as some reading and writing challenges.

Language for Communication

Students on the spectrum may or may not experience the standard types of speech and language challenges described above, but for them, other communication challenges are more universal, setting them apart from their peers and profoundly affecting the ways they interact with others. For the most part, these communication challenges fall into the categories of semantics and pragmatics.

Semantics. These are rules that govern the meaning we assign to words. The use of semantics is a particular trouble spot for students on the autism spectrum because word meanings tend to be fluid, whereas these students tend to interpret them consistently in straightforward, fixed, and concrete ways.

Pragmatics. The subtext of language is called pragmatics. It's about how we say what we say and what we really mean. This layer of communication consists of two primary components: *nonverbal* communication, or body language, which includes facial expression, gestures, body posture, and body position; and *paraverbal* communication, which relates to the speaker's pitch, volume, intonation, rate, rhythm, and emphasis. The use of nonverbal and paraverbal cues greatly influences the meaning and interpretation of communication.

What follows are some of the common semantic and pragmatic challenges that most profoundly affect the communication abilities of students on the spectrum.

Echolalia

Echolalia, which is a semantic challenge, is the repetition of the words of others. Although echolalia can occur as a passing phase in any child's early language development, it is most common and enduring among students on the spectrum. It can occur in two forms.

Immediate echolalia. This is the repetition of words just heard. A student who is asked, "Are you ready?" and responds, "You ready," is exhibiting immediate echolalia.

Delayed echolalia. This is the repetition of words heard at another time—during a movie or television commercial, for example. Students who use familiar phrases, like "Just keep swimming, just keep swimming" or "Who you gonna call? Ghostbusters!" are demonstrating delayed echolalia. Delayed echolalia, sometimes known as "scripting," often involves repetition of the same lines or phrases over and over. In that sense, it serves as a comfort anchor, providing students with the reliable comfort of familiarity.

Although both forms of echolalia can seem non-communicative or indicative of a lack of comprehension, echolalia may at times actually be an important communication tool for students on the spectrum. Some students use it as a way of maintaining social interaction when they don't know what to say or cannot express the words they are thinking. For them, repetition of something previously heard can become a default, go-to response.

Alternatively, students may adopt a certain expression to convey a particular emotion or experience. For example, a student who is muttering, "Just keep swimming," may be engaging in a form of self-talk, a way of prompting persistence and patience. This can also communicate to others that frustration is building. So, although echolalic expressions may appear to be meaningless, it is important for educators to spend some time working to decipher their origin and their possible function for the students who use them. If the students themselves cannot explain these expressions, their parents and guardians are the next best resource for this kind of information.

Echolalia should not be confused with *perseveration,* the repetition of a particular concept, word, phrase, action, or routine that is in the forefront of a student's mind. Perseveration may cause students to think about, talk about, or play-act the same topics endlessly. Students may to try to engage others in repetitive and circumscribed conversations that relate to their perseverative area of interest. (Read more about perseveration in Chapter 6.)

Prosody

Prosody, which is a component of paraverbal communication, pertains to the rhythm and tone of language. Some students who are on the autism spectrum often have trouble modulating their own prosody, which means that their language and affect while speaking may be flat—devoid of emphasis or emotion.

Multiple Meanings

Another semantic challenge faced by students on the spectrum is fluidity of meaning. A crucial element of the social code of tweendom and adolescence is getting the joke. And a big part of getting the joke is reading between the lines and recognizing that individual words can have very different meanings. For example, students who don't understand why everyone giggles when one teacher is heard telling another, "I have recess duty today," or why everyone laughs when Taylor innocently asks, "Can I have one of your balls?" can quickly become ostracized.

Abstraction

As neurotypical students grow, they develop an ability to understand abstract concepts. However, most students on the spectrum struggle greatly with this. Language that is not straightforward—similes, metaphors, idioms, jokes, and proverbs—is commonly lost on students on the spectrum, who can have a hard time making sense of even direct statements. On the other hand, once idiomatic language is specifically explained to students on the spectrum, they often find the unexpected use of language to be hilarious, as they remain focused on the literal meaning. My son always gets a kick (if you will) out of idioms that depict ridiculous images like "Let's hit the road" and "When pigs fly" or the anatomical anomalies implied by "I'm all ears" and "I've got your back."

Joint Attention and Social Reciprocity

Now let's delve into some aspects of communication that have nothing to do with words. These social components of communication are common areas of challenge for students on the spectrum and significantly inhibit their ability to connect with and relate to peers as well as adults.

Joint attention is the desire to seek shared experience with others. Even as infants, babies point to a shiny or similarly diverting object to share the thrill of it with a caregiver. Toddlers drag their teacher to the easel to share pride in their latest masterpiece. Students on the autism spectrum, however, even as they grow, do not tend to be inherently motivated to seek out shared experience. They are more likely to be content occupying themselves, without the need for social approbation.

In the early childhood and early elementary school years, interactive skills are expectably limited, and even neurotypical children may not seek social connections. When young children are drawn to play together, they play alongside each other rather than with each other. This "parallel play" is developmentally right on track—in the early years. Accordingly, conversation at this age is quite concrete: one student says, "I had oatmeal for breakfast," and another says, "Oh," and that, unequivocally, constitutes a conversation. These early conversations and interactions follow individual trajectories and lack the *social reciprocity* necessary to blossom fluidly into more complex interactions. Even in these early stages of social development, however, many students on the spectrum may already be showing deficits or idiosyncrasies in their social motivation, social approach, and social referencing.

In the upper elementary grades, neurotypical students make the developmental leap from parallel play to interactive play, from egocentric conversation to reciprocal conversation, and from straightforward, fact-based language to nuanced innuendo. From this point on, socialization requires flexibility, spontaneity, sharing, turn taking, patience, and reading between the lines. Communication becomes layered with nonverbal and paraverbal cues. Now, even those students on the spectrum who had been managing fairly well in the realms of parallel play and concrete conversation begin to struggle. They remain literal thinkers. Right around 3rd grade—just as the curriculum shifts from the concrete (which is in their wheelhouse) to the abstract (which is not), and just as "learning to read" evolves into "reading to learn"— the social challenges of these students suddenly become apparent.

Students on the spectrum are likely to misinterpret or even entirely overlook crucial elements of nonverbal communication such as eye rolls, kicks under the table, or loaded glances or glares, and elements of paraverbal communication such as sarcasm, impatience, condescension, and even kindness and sincerity—all crucial components of social acceptance in an inclusive setting.

For example, one day, Ben, a middle school student on the spectrum, told his classmate Attib, "I like your backpack. Can I have it?"

Attib rolled his eyes and grunted, "Yeah, right."

Like most students on the spectrum, Ben clings to rigid conversational rules and expectations and accepts comments at face value. To him, the expression, "Yeah, right," is composed of two affirmative words: *yeah* and *right*. Absent any understanding of the nonverbal and paraverbal mitigating factors (in this case, Attib's eye roll and sarcastic grunt), "Yeah, right" sounds like a fully agreeable response. As Ben grabbed Attib's backpack and slung it over his own shoulder, he had no idea why Attib and his friends started hollering.

Mindblindness

It's not only Ben's poor understanding of nonverbal and paraverbal communication that causes him to believe it's fine to take Attib's backpack. Ben has also failed to intuit that Attib would want to keep his own backpack, that the backpack is a thing of value to Attib. This is because Ben, like most students on the spectrum, also struggles with a challenge called *mindblindness,* which is the inability to take the perspective of another person. Also known as "theory of mind," mindblindness causes students to have difficulty anticipating the effect that their own words or actions will have on others. Mindblindness is one of the hallmark features of autism, and often one of the most intractable.

Developmentally, typical toddlers and preschoolers tend to be rather egocentric. The ability to take the perspective of others is a cognitive-behavioral trait actively cultivated by early childhood teachers. By early elementary school, an awareness and consideration of others emerges in typical students that may not bloom in students on the spectrum.

Students who struggle with mindblindness cannot decode the eye roll, the kick under the table, the cringe. They may keep talking at you, even when you're doubled over having a coughing fit. They may see no reason to share toys or tools, because they don't stop to consider the needs of others. They may see no reason to be polite, because they don't recognize that their words can affect others. Mindblindness can make it very hard for these students to be responsive to or respectful of other people's feelings. And that can make it hard for other students to enjoy their company.

Empathy

Although in years past, individuals on the autism spectrum were thought to lack empathy altogether, that notion is no longer accepted (Brewer & Murphy, 2016). Fact is, folks with autism can be extraordinarily empathic, kind, and affectionate. But empathy is widely considered to be a three-step *process,* and students on the spectrum may indeed stumble on at least one of those steps. Let's take a closer look.

Step 1: Cognitive empathy. When neurotypical individuals engage in socially reciprocal interactions, we take note of the feelings or reactions of our conversational partner. Whether we do this consciously or subconsciously, it's important that we notice that our friend is having feelings and reactions throughout the interaction so that we can adjust our contributions accordingly. As we speak or act, we tend to decode the information we get from other people's faces and body language. If our friend cringes, we note it and infer that we may have struck a nerve. If our friend laughs, we note it and infer that they are enjoying what we are saying. If our friend falls and cries out, we note it and infer that they may be hurt. And if our friend looks at the clock, sighs repeatedly, and shifts from foot to foot, we note it and infer that they've had enough.

Students on the spectrum can have significant difficulty with this cognitive process because it's not concrete and is rarely straightforward. Recognizing what another person is feeling means not only being able to decode their tone and body language but also being able to discern meaning even when the words are not straightforward or don't match the speaker's tone of voice or facial expressions.

Moreover, students on the spectrum are likely to assume that other people know what they themselves know, think what they are thinking, feel what they are feeling, and are interested in whatever interests them. Thanks to mindblindness, these erroneous assumptions lead to frequent conversational difficulties. My 21-year-old son and I get tangled in conversations like this one almost daily:

> **Me:** Where are you going?
>
> **Him:** You already know.
>
> **Me:** No, I don't. If I already knew, I wouldn't be asking. Where are you going?
>
> **Him, exasperated:** Mom! You already know this!
>
> **Me:** I don't know all the same things you know. Just tell me where you're going. Then I will know.
>
> **Him, grumbling:** Fine. I'm going to get pizza. But I don't know how you didn't already know that.

Step 2: Affective empathy. The second component of empathy is *affective empathy*, which is the ability to relate to what others are feeling. For most of us, affective empathy follows naturally from cognitive empathy; as soon as we notice and decode what someone else is feeling, to a certain extent, we tend to slide into that same space with them. A healthy dose of affective empathy leads us to relate to the feelings of others by guiding us to tap into times when we felt similarly. But for students on the spectrum, mindblindness again gets in the way.

Step 3: Expressive empathy. The third component of empathy, often called "compassionate empathy," is the step that leads us to act on behalf of others. Now that we have identified the feeling being communicated, and we have related to what the experience of that feeling may be like, *expressive empathy* guides us to do something.

For example, when we have identified and related to a cringe, we apologize, explain, or change course. When we have identified and related to a laugh, we double down on the joke or we laugh along. When we have identified and related to pain, we try to help. And when we have identified and related to impatience, we wrap up the story (Bariso, 2018).

Students on the spectrum cannot readily scale the steps of the multistage process that is empathy, and that's why they can appear to be uncaring. But it's not for lack of feeling; it's for lack of skill. As soon as we break the process down and teach these students how to decode facial expressions and body language, how to relate to feelings, and how to act on feelings, kindness and compassion are right there. Indeed, most students on the spectrum feel deeply for the plights of others as soon as they learn to read the signals.

To me, affective empathy is the heart of empathy, both literally and figuratively; it is both the emotional center of empathy and, I believe, its core component. Students on the spectrum tend to get stuck on the cognitive decoding step that leads to the feelings, and so they may not reach the affective step on their own. And even if they do reach the affective step, they may not be able to make sense of what they are feeling or perceiving or what to do about it. But without exception, I have found that the compassion is there, the kindness is there. These students only need help accessing it. We may just have to build a ramp.

The Hidden Social Curriculum

Empathy and other forms of "alt-verbal communication," like nonverbal and paraverbal cues, are not usually taught. We tend to expect students and adults to just know them. For example, can you recall anyone ever actually teaching you that when the person you're talking to starts looking at the clock, they're ready to end the conversation? More than likely, you figured this out on your own. It's a code, and you deciphered it.

Coded information like this is commonly known as the *hidden curriculum,* a broad set of unwritten, untaught expectations that we assume others will just know. Students who are not aware of the hidden social curriculum would not know the kid code, which presumes that, for example, telling dirty jokes is cool only when there are no adults around, or that teachers don't always have to be told when someone breaks a rule. Students who overlook information like this would also be unable to infer which classmates are likely to be kind and which are likely to be cruel.

Beyond the unspoken rules of socialization, the hidden curriculum is a part of academic and behavioral expectations, too. Has anyone clarified for these literal students that when the teacher says, "OK, you may now open your test books," it means that they can actually begin testing? Has anyone actually explained to students that it's acceptable to hold hands with the teacher in 1st grade but not in 7th grade?

Maybe you've noticed that when raucous behaviors arise, your very arrival on the scene as an administrator is usually enough to redirect the actions of neurotypical students. That's because you inhabit a position that is imbued with authority. But the implications of your position may not be intuited by students on the spectrum. Even your physical stance—solemn-faced, arms crossed—may not convey to them the seriousness of your expectation. And even when you repeat your expectation in a louder voice, your escalating volume and tone may not communicate to these students that you're at the end of your rope.

In situations like this—when you find students on the spectrum continuing to go about their loud or raucous business even after you feel you've made your disapproval clear—don't assume malice or defiance; instead, assume non-comprehension. Whereas most students infer meaning spontaneously from these body postures, inflections, and other contextual elements, those implied meanings need to be overtly taught to students on the spectrum.

As an example, consider the experience of 8-year-old Jeannie when she joined an inclusive softball team. Jeannie had not played softball before. There was a weekend pick-up game in her neighborhood, but, because of her social differences, she had never been invited or able to join. Since Jeannie is on the autism spectrum, her parents met with the coach to explain that Jeannie would need instructions simplified and made very clear. They asked the coach to check for understanding by having Jeannie repeat the instructions back in her own words. And just to be extra-careful, her parents taught Jeannie the fundamental rules of the game in advance—what and where the bases are, how to run the bases, what counts as a strike, what constitutes an out, and so on.

When Jeannie took her first turn at bat, she struck out . . . and remained standing in ready position at home plate, bat over her shoulder, waiting to receive another pitch. The coach informed her that she was out. "Yes, I know," Jeannie answered matter-of-factly. "I got three strikes, so I'm out." And yet, there she remained, standing at the plate. Her mother, watching from the sidelines, recognized the disconnect. They had all forgotten to explain to Jeannie what being "out" *implied*. Jeannie's mother called, "Being out means your turn's over, Jeannie. Put down the bat and go sit on the bench."

In this situation, despite her parents' diligent efforts, Jeannie encountered a set of expectations that had not been taught or scripted for her with quite enough specificity. And even though she had seen many of her teammates get called "out" and retire to the bench, she had not spontaneously made use of those context clues and did not intuit that she should follow suit.

Leading the Way to Successful Inclusion

Helping students who are on the spectrum learn to decode the hidden curriculum is crucial to their success in an inclusive environment and especially in an inclusion classroom. To keep up socially—and academically, too—they need to learn to use and understand elements of language and communication in ways that don't come naturally to them. In this next section, we will explore both individual and schoolwide approaches to boosting language and communication skills to support socialization.

Supporting Communication

As mentioned in Chapter 2, special education teachers working in self-contained classrooms often incorporate visual communication systems to facilitate interaction with students who are nonverbal, minimally verbal, or otherwise language challenged. These same tools can be beneficial in an inclusion classroom.

Communication Systems

Commonly known as PC (picture-communication) systems or PECS (picture exchange communication systems), these systems utilize cards that feature symbols or icons and can be exchanged from hand to hand or displayed using Velcro or magnets. The reciprocal use of these simple, straightforward cards promotes comprehension as well as interaction and engagement. Students on the spectrum benefit from using these specially designed, laminated cards to help communicate their needs, thoughts, and feelings; educators can use the cards to help communicate expectations. It's not uncommon for special ed teachers to actually wear a book of symbols for easy access at all times. As needed, individual students may have their own set, specifically curated to meet their own practical and expressive needs.

Instructional Technology

Many classrooms today provide all students with technology resources that open new worlds of communication for everyone.

The very same instructional technology you already use with your typically functioning students can go a long way toward supporting the communication and socialization of students on the spectrum. This includes everyday tech tools, such as tablets, laptops, file sharing programs, interactive whiteboards, document cameras, remote response systems, digital cameras, multimedia presentation programs, interactive books and magazines, interactive math programs, makerspaces, and of course, all of the vast content resources of the internet.

Assistive Technology

Assistive technology supports the needs of students who are unable to access the curriculum via conventional means. When needed, these supports are specified in a student's individualized education program (IEP) and must be provided. Just as students who are deaf cannot be asked to "listen harder," students with certain identified learning challenges cannot circumvent their challenges simply by trying or working harder. They need adaptations made to the learning environment in order to allow them access to it. Assistive technology that supports communication is called *augmentative and alternative communication* (AAC). Exciting new AAC technology is being created every day and can range from low tech to high tech. Commonly used AAC for students on the spectrum today include the following:

- *Highlighter strips* can be placed on a page of text, highlighting and drawing focus to the section that requires attention while also concealing extraneous information on a page.
- *Text-to-speech technology,* sometimes known as "speech generating devices" (SGDs), allows nonverbal students and others with significant speech challenges to communicate verbally by translating their written words into spoken communication.

- *Speech-to-text technology* allows students who struggle to express their thoughts in writing (due to motor or processing challenges) to do so by translating their spoken words into written text.
- *Word prediction software* helps students who struggle with word retrieval by scanning the context of writing and suggesting relevant words.
- *Smartpens* record and digitize spoken and handwritten text, allowing students to revisit class lessons and to organize and search within their notes.
- *Apps* designed to support language and communication can be used on tablets and other mobile devices to facilitate socialization in the classroom.

Assistive technology does not diminish students' efforts to use conventional forms of communication and socialization. Instead, it helps students begin to perceive themselves as communicators, which inspires them to continue working on developing their conventional communication skills. When appropriately utilized, these devices and other technology tools augment students' ability to interact with the learning environment by facilitating independence, bolstering success, building confidence, reducing frustration, and improving behavior. Today, a mind-boggling (but ultimately mind-organizing!) array of digital programs are available that support comprehension and engagement and serve as scaffolding tools to help move students forward.

Supporting Social Development

When you and your teachers take the time to examine your language, instructions, and expectations, and carefully peel away all the layers of the hidden curriculum, you are likely to uncover eager students on the spectrum who are more than happy to comply.

Elements of the hidden curriculum are so deeply embedded in daily life that it can be difficult for supporters of students on the spectrum to spot them all. Here are some strategies to help unmask the hidden curriculum for students on the spectrum.

Social Perspective Taking

Mindblindness, as its name suggests, contributes to the invisibility of the hidden social curriculum to students on the spectrum. But in inclusive settings, students can learn to see in all kinds of new ways. Social perspective taking is a crucial component of empathy, kindness, flexibility, patience, and lots of other skills that determine social success.

In his article "Emotional Intelligence: Learning to Walk in Another's Shoes," Hunter Gehlbach (2017) describes three priorities for teaching social perspective taking at any grade level.

Make it a habit to ask for multiple perspectives. Gehlbach recommends that educators avoid implying that there is one right answer to any question. For example, rather than ask students, "Why did the Loyalists resist seeking independence from Britain?" teachers might ask a more open-ended question, such as "What are some possible reasons that the Loyalists resisted seeking independence from Britain?"

Students on the spectrum tend to lock into ideas and opinions, just as they lock into their routines. To support development of social perspective taking, teachers need to make a concerted effort to encourage a growth mindset with these students across all contexts. The goal is to help them internalize that an automatic or "gut" reaction is not fixed and final; it's only the beginning. Accordingly, teachers should guide students through the process of developing an opinion. Tools such as graphic organizers can help them explore all the considerations that go into forming an opinion: gathering facts, reflecting on facts, consulting with other people (which includes listening to, discussing, and considering their input), updating information, and so on. Note, too, that carrying out these steps relies on executive function skills (described in Chapter 3), so the individual components of these steps may need to be taught along the way.

A simple shift to more open-ended questioning shows students that there is more than one right answer, that different people may view situations in different ways, and that it's just fine to be uncertain. It shows them that possibilities—not just certainties—are welcome and that multiple viewpoints are a good thing.

Encourage students to be social detectives, not judges. Gehlbach suggests that teachers lead discussions of the various viewpoints that emerge from members of the class. This guides students to practice listening openly and respectfully to other perspectives and explaining their own perspectives.

If students have difficulty with this task, teachers might use role-play to help them adopt the perspectives of other people. For example, the history teacher might make this process concrete by giving students props and costume pieces to help them to—perhaps literally—step into another person's shoes.

Provide opportunities for feedback as students learn to read others' perspectives. Inclusion teachers can be upfront about the fact that this lesson is about both content and social skills. For example, a middle school history teacher might say this: "While we are learning about the events leading up to the American Revolution, we will also be learning to respect the fact that different people have different ideas and opinions." Or, "Alejandro and Maia have both made interesting points. Alejandro, how might Maia's ideas influence or change your thinking?"

As students share differing opinions, the teacher can easily provide feedback as to how well they are doing—not only in terms of the content but also in terms of learning to respect each other's perspectives.

The High Value of Low Stakes: Social Skills Groups

Gehlbach notes that students need "many low-stakes opportunities to practice social perspective taking" (2017, p. 11), ideally in an open and trusting environment in which mistakes are expected and feedback is provided. Taking risks is not a comfortable experience for students on the spectrum, who generally want to know exactly what to expect before embarking on any activity. The workaround for teachers is to cultivate a community in which mistakes are explicitly celebrated as learning experiences.

To that end, social skills groups are indispensable to the social development of almost all students on the spectrum. In these groups, which meet outside the classroom, skills can be taught, retaught, and practiced in a supported environment that is specifically designed for social learning. School counselors and speech-language pathologists are well suited to run groups like these; in the best circumstances, they will team up to run a social skills group together. Social skills groups can be mandated weekly and provided as part of a school day or held at lunchtime. But many schools simply do not provide groups like these. Do whatever you can to support and encourage the implementation and continuation of social skills groups. They can make all the difference to the success of your inclusive program.

Reading the Room

As noted, students on the autism spectrum, struggling with anxiety and faced with a baffling hidden curriculum, tend to rely on a rigid set of rote skills to guide their functioning across contexts. Rather than adapt their approach to specific situations, they are likely to apply a singular, learned behavior to a variety of situations. This is why a student on the spectrum returning from the resource room may burst into the classroom exuberantly proclaiming, "I'm back!" regardless of whether the class is currently bustling with a noisy activity or hushed for silent reading. Because they don't naturally pick up on the cues that dictate communication and social behavior in different circumstances, students on the spectrum need guidance to learn how to read a room and adapt their communication and their social approach.

Remember, icons can be added at opportune places on their schedules that remind them to stop, look, and listen before proceeding. Students who have particular trouble with this may need a mini-schedule that prompts them to stop, look, and listen whenever they approach any new situation. But once they've stopped, looked, and listened, what are they to make of what they observe? Interpreting the meaning of the cues observed is part of the hidden curriculum.

Teachers, speech-language pathologists, and counselors can help students on the spectrum learn about different environments and the specific communication and social-behavior expectations of each. Then they can teach specific communication and social-behavioral strategies to use in specific situations. For example, a lesson might focus on teaching the social expectation that everyone enters a classroom quietly so as not to disrupt work going on inside. For some students on the spectrum, that cognitive-behavioral lesson (perhaps repeated many times) may be sufficient to guide their behavior in future situations. Other students may need more than conceptual education and guidance; they may need a script—a simple, specific set of rules for certain circumstances—that they can memorize and follow by rote.

Reading Feelings

Another valuable strategy for supporting the communication and socialization skills of students on the spectrum is teaching them to recognize emotional signposts—cues that serve as indicators of feelings or mood. Emotional signposts include nonverbal cues such as tears (as indicative of emotional or physical pain), rolled eyes (as indicative of annoyance), smirks (as indicative of sarcasm), twinkling eyes (as indicative of playfulness), and so on.

These interpretations come so spontaneously to many people that it's hard to imagine having to teach them and harder still to explain them. Classroom teachers, speech-language pathologists, and counselors can use emotion posters, mirrors, apps, and even emojis to help students learn to decode the messages that appear on other people's faces and in their body language. These strategies help students access their cognitive empathy.

But once students on the spectrum have learned to identify the meaning of the signposts they see and hear, what are they to do about it? How do they go on to access affective and expressive empathy? Many students benefit from role-play; sometimes they truly cannot fathom what someone else might be feeling until they are guided to specifically imagine or even project themselves into the same circumstances. Teachers, speech-language pathologists, and counselors do a lot of this kind of work with students—not only guiding them through role-play scenarios but also debriefing what they learn from the experience. These lessons need to be made explicit and brought fully into consciousness to support learning. Students should be guided to consider how they would feel in a certain situation, how they would feel about the different ways others might respond to them, and what they can do in the future to be a good friend.

Other students may not be able to engage in this kind of cognitive-behavioral work. They may need to be provided with a set of prompts that indicate which facial expressions or feelings in others should generate what responses from them.

Social Stories

One of the most effective tools for helping students figure out what to do in challenging situations and how to respond to complicated feelings is the social story.

First developed by educator Carol Gray, social stories are short, fact-based narratives that break down complex situations (such as waiting in line, doing homework, staying calm, and taking turns), validate the challenges within, and then guide coping skills and reactions (Gray, 2015). Social stories are written to convey empathic support and encouragement, empowering students with the skills and confidence they need to succeed.

Gray presents a very specific, 10-part formula for writing these stories that includes starting from the student's perspective, expanding to include other perspectives, and ending with a positive outcome. She and others have created hundreds of social stories that can be purchased and broadly applied. But social stories work best when customized to address individual students' comprehension levels, metacognitive awareness, functioning styles, coping skills, and specific reactions to given events. Stories can be written for—or, better yet, *with*—students who need them. Figure 5.1 shows an example.

Figure 5.1: Kele's Social Story

How to Greet Someone

There are many ways to greet someone.

When I see someone I know, especially if I am seeing that person for the first time that day, it's friendly to say "hello." They may say "hello," too. They may stop to talk with me.

Sometimes people shake hands to say "hello." Usually it is adults who shake hands to say "hello." For example, an adult may try to shake my hand if he or she is meeting me for the first time. This will happen more and more as I get older.

Once in a while, I go to visit relatives or close friends. A short hug as I arrive means hello.

Sometimes, if I am just passing someone I know, I may smile, wave, or just nod my head. If I said hello to that person earlier in the day, smiling, waving, or nodding my head means, Hello again. This is a friendly thing to do.

There are many ways to greet someone. I may think of other ways that people greet one another!

Source: From *The New Social Story Book, 15th Anniversary Edition* (p. 145) by C. Gray, 2015, Arlington, TX: Future Horizons, Inc. Copyright 2015 by Future Horizons, Inc. Reprinted with permission.

School counselors, special education teachers, and speech-language pathologists can be recruited and trained to help write a social story for or with a student. There are even apps to guide social story development. Relevant social stories can be attached to an individual student's desk or a designated folder, copied and sent home, reviewed every day, or consulted as needed.

Supporting Socialization Outside the Classroom

Socialization, outside the structured and predictable environment of the classroom, is survival of the fittest. In addition to guiding your teachers to create classroom spaces that are socially and emotionally mindful and instructive, you're going to have to pay close attention to the safety and comfort of students on the spectrum when they are in less supervised social spaces.

Lunch, Recess, and Free Time

The unstructured parts of the school day that are the favorites of many students can be the most challenging parts of the day for students on the spectrum in inclusive programs. Lunch presents all kinds of sensory overload, and recess is a social free-for-all. Consider that the very purpose of free time is a reprieve from structure: *Here's some free time! Get up and go!* But for students on the spectrum, a break from structure is no reprieve; it's sensory assault and social agony. There are no assigned places to be, no inside voices, no designated partners, no activity schedules, no fixed rules.

In the lunchroom and outdoors, carefully calibrated student-teacher ratios vanish as all kinds of students are thrown together in large numbers, usually without the supervision of autism-educated adults. This is prime time for bullies, and your students on the spectrum—with their blatant idiosyncrasies and social naiveté—are especially vulnerable. In the environment where these students need the most support, the least support is provided.

Outdoor activities are often organized and mediated by students on their own. While negotiating the rules of a pick-up kickball game often presents important learning opportunities for most neurotypical students, it can create a multitude of challenging situations for others—especially for students on the spectrum. It's no wonder that many times students on the spectrum can be found hovering on the periphery during recess, trying to keep away from the hub of noise and chaos, possibly feeling left out, or perhaps relishing the relative peacefulness of a quieter corner.

There are a number of things you can do as an administrator to make these inclusive settings safer and more welcoming for students on the spectrum and also help them build social and communication skills:

- Alert cafeteria and free-time monitors about students who may need some extra support, and guide them to keep an eye out and to intervene gently when necessary.

- Ask speech-language pathologists or occupational therapists to schedule push-in sessions with these students during lunchtime or recess. Providers can use the sessions to set up interactive group games or other activities on the playground. These activities can then be supervised by lunch or recess aides on days when therapy is not on the schedule.

- Allow students on the spectrum to go to the lunchroom a few minutes before the lunch rush to avoid the line and find seats while the environment is still calm.

- Find or create quieter, calmer places for students on the spectrum to eat if the cafeteria space is overstimulating to them.

- Consider whether students on the spectrum who find free time overwhelming or socially stressful could be positioned as helpers for younger groups at recess (a win-win!).

- Provide lunchroom and free-time staff with copies of the Fact & Tip sheet for building and bus staff on pp. 177–178, a resource created specifically for their purposes.

Peer Participation

Another helpful strategy for easing the social and communication challenges students on the spectrum face is to recruit peers to provide support. There are a number of ways to facilitate engagement between your students on the spectrum and their neurotypical peers while building both groups' empathy and social skills.

Circle of friends (Schlieder, 2007) is a popular framework for building peer support for students on the spectrum in inclusive settings. A circle of friends is a group of designated peers who participate in supervised lunch and activity groups with students on the spectrum, playing games and practicing social skills, such as making conversation and taking turns. These types of structured groups offer students on the spectrum safe opportunities to practice socializing and be part of a peer group. Moreover, the relationships formed during these structured activities tend to carry over beyond lunchtime and recess, creating new circles of friends and supporters for all students involved.

Peers who have been recruited for this purpose also serve a valuable role as eyes and ears outside of the classroom. They can look out for vulnerable students and let you or teachers know when they see unkind behavior toward them in the hallways, on the bus, in the bathroom, and elsewhere.

Consider these various potential incarnations of peer support networks:

- At the elementary level, appoint "companions of the day" to partner up with specific students for small-group projects, walking in the hall, or any other suitable activities.

- At the secondary level, develop a squad of trustworthy student volunteers to seek out any students who are alone. Volunteers can sit with vulnerable students at lunch and engage with them or help them join activities during other unstructured time. Give volunteers some strategies to engage reluctant peers. Remind them that even though their identified classmates have challenges, they are first and foremost individuals with feelings and opinions that must be respected. Despite volunteers' best efforts, students on the spectrum may not always be receptive to social overtures; teach volunteers to respect a peer's right to make choices for themselves, and to try again at other times.

- Offer students on the spectrum opportunities to help or mentor others. Maybe they can turn the jump rope, play catch with the kindergartners during recess (as suggested previously), or carry books for a peer who has a broken arm. Perhaps they can quiz peers on their multiplication tables or help them locate books on the library shelves.

Developing peer support networks benefits all the students in an inclusive school. Janet Ferone, founding administrator of alternative and inclusion programs for Boston Public Schools, emphasizes the importance of making sure that both parties "feel equal in the relationship and that general education students are not helping out of charity or feeling bad for the special education students." As she explained to me:

While it is hard to quantify the benefits of peer support, just looking around the cafeteria and seeing students who have clearly visible stims, twirling and flapping next to their general education peers with no one batting an eyelash, is rewarding on both ends. We have had students intern with students on the autism spectrum, and they report feeling that they've learned more than the students they came in to help.

The Battle Against Bullying

Students on the spectrum are prime targets for bullying in inclusive programs. Their awkward or "clueless" social behaviors can leave them vulnerable to teasing, aggression, and rejection. Plus, their limited capacity for self-regulation makes them likely to get upset in dramatic ways that are gratifying and encouraging to bullies.

Setting an Inclusive Tone: Beyond the Bells

Conveying a message that after-school clubs are "welcoming" to students on the spectrum sounds great but doesn't mean much. While a warm welcome is lovely, it's not nearly enough to support the social and communication needs of students on the spectrum in a group setting. Their involvement needs to be *facilitated* every step of the way.

Be sure to have inclusive supports like these readily and explicitly available for every after-school activity to make it possible for students on the spectrum to participate:

- Peer escorts to help them find the meeting
- Peer buddies to help them out during the activities
- Advisors or peers who regularly verify that they understand instructions and plans and that they receive and process all relevant information and communications
- Advisors, assistants, or paraprofessionals who attend the group full-time to guide and facilitate interactions among peers throughout the activities

Students on the spectrum and others who may be bullied should be taught preventive measures to help them stay safe. Here are a few valuable strategies to pass along to your staff and to reinforce schoolwide:

- *Steer clear.* Students on the spectrum should be *taught* to steer clear of kids who bully. This may sound obvious to you, but students on the spectrum may not intuit that proximity to bullies increases the likelihood of negative interactions. Be sure that this information is explained clearly to vulnerable students.

- *Stay in view.* Adults bear the responsibility for ensuring a bully-free environment, but they can't monitor what they can't see. Teachers or monitors often give the warning "Stay where I can see you." However, mindblindness makes it almost impossible for students on the spectrum to be able to figure out that multifaceted perspective: *How can I know where you can see me?* A much clearer instruction from an adult is one that takes the student's perspective: "Stay where you can see me."

- *Find a buddy.* There is safety in numbers. Explain to students on the spectrum that whenever they find that adults are out of view, they should find a buddy to stick with until an adult is present. Help students identify suitable peers who would be good choices to approach for help. This is where companion arrangements or school- or classroom-based peer support network systems can be very valuable, ensuring that there are plenty of vetted sources of support on hand for students on the spectrum and for anyone else who might be a target for bullies.

Making Group Work *Work*

Communication and socialization are also necessary skills for successful collaborative group work. Navigating the social and communication demands of group work in an inclusion classroom is fraught with challenges for students on the spectrum well before they can even address the actual content.

The moment a teacher announces, "Break up into groups," the volume in the room ramps up. Classmates are now rearranging themselves and their chairs—talking, laughing, debating, and negotiating group membership and roles. Friends seek each other out, and students who may have fewer friends and less developed social skills can easily find themselves untethered. Plus, amid the sensory and social onslaught, an entirely new set of rules and expectations takes over.

The traditional approach to group work is experiential: tell kids to get into groups and let them figure it out. This is commonly believed to be a necessary learning experience for neurotypical students (just like mediating their own kickball games, as mentioned previously), but students on the spectrum are unlikely to have the requisite skills necessary to rise to this challenge. In the context of the executive function, sensory, and social challenges discussed in this book, consider the inherent obstacles they face when it's time to work in groups:

- *Self-selection.* Many teachers instruct students to form their own groups, which means that students on the spectrum need to recognize peers who can be trusted to be kind and approach them in socially expectable ways—nuanced challenges that require social sophistication.

- *Collaboration.* The defining feature of group work is collaboration, which requires students to take turns, share resources, and tolerate mistakes, as well as access the patience and the flexibility to consider and accept others' ideas— all of which are challenging social as well as executive function skills.

- *Communication.* Sharing ideas and answers in articulate, respectful, and timely ways is especially challenging without the support of a teacher to designate who gets to speak, when, and for how long.

- *Negotiating and understanding roles and rules.* Now that it's no longer clear who is in charge, students on the spectrum can be confused and overwhelmed by the anarchy and not know where to turn to address problems. They are often resistant to the seemingly inexplicable emergence of new rules and new peer leaders who determine the group's agenda and assign jobs and tasks.

All of these issues can pose a particular problem in special areas, such as art, music, and physical education (PE), and in sports, where sensory challenges abound and groups, ensembles, and teams are par for the course. The reproducible Fact & Tip sheets for special area teachers (pp. 173–174) and for PE teachers and coaches (pp. 179–180), included in the Appendix, are designed to address specific issues that arise in those contexts. Please share them with your special area and PE teachers and with all others who work with students on the spectrum.

In any class where group work is expected, it should be taught—like any other skill teachers expect students to use in class. Encourage every teacher to give a lesson on group work that defines the different roles in groups (e.g., leader, note taker, timekeeper, reporter, equipment distributor and collector, art critic, music critic, efficiency expert, fact checker) and lays out the specific task expectations within each role. Teachers should show students how to set group goals and prioritize activities, provide strategies for resolving conflict, and delineate how and when to get help. It's also helpful for teachers to write out and distribute group expectations so that students can refer to them as they work and whenever they need a reminder.

Supporting Social Acceptance

As hard as it is for students on the spectrum to make sense of their typical peers, it's equally hard for their peers to make sense of them. As discussed previously, beginning in late elementary school and continuing through middle and high school, typical peers become increasingly socially savvy and aware of social differences. Social know-how becomes a litmus test for popularity, and peers begin to split off on the basis of who can pick up on sarcasm and innuendo, and who can't. Typical peers in inclusive classrooms have to go more than halfway to have a relationship with students on the spectrum, and many are not interested in doing that. It's easier to be friends with someone who shares your interests, takes turns playing, is flexible, gets your jokes, and respects your feelings. And so students on the autism spectrum get left out or bullied.

Students on the spectrum whose challenges are external and readily apparent to peers—that is, those who flap, rock, or make noises—may engender spontaneous indulgence in the form of patience and kindness from peers. Alternatively, their overt challenges may lead unenlightened or unkind peers to assume, incorrectly, that affected students won't notice or feel the effects of pranks and cruel words.

Students on the autism spectrum whose symptoms are more internal than external, however, face a different kind of social challenge. In the absence of obvious differences, like stims or speech impediments, these students tend to be viewed as essentially typical, and so their social idiosyncrasies are even more unexpected. Peers are likely to cut them less slack, and their social challenges are often perceived as rudeness or weirdness rather than as indicators of a disability. This is a common double-edged sword for students whose symptoms are primarily internal.

A school leader's best response to these realities is to create and maintain a school culture that promotes acceptance and inclusion.

Build Inclusive Knowledge

As an inclusive education leader, you set the tone for the school, the district, and the community. Bring in speakers to educate your entire faculty, staff, and student population about autism. Try to make inclusivity a priority for in-service learning and assemblies. Bring in programs that exemplify all kinds of diversity and adversity—not only speakers who address autism but also speakers who have overcome drug addiction or who are living with mental illness or who are survivors of domestic abuse or violence or who are transgender or who rose up from poverty or homelessness. Promote firsthand awareness of all kinds of people and all kinds of challenges, circumstances, struggles, supports, and triumph. Model inclusivity by including all members of the faculty and staff in these programs so that everyone in the building is on board with inclusion.

Be sure to include every single member of the faculty and staff in whatever autism trainings and supports you provide. Facilitate the sharing of resources and strategies to include special area teachers, therapists, and building staff and bus staff to the extent that effective strategies might be helpful. Providing information and support and obtaining buy-in from everyone in the building create a seamless environment of inclusivity and a team of champions for our students on the spectrum. Share the reproducible Inclusion Myths and Facts guide (see pp. 165–166) with all families to spread accurate information and dispel common concerns.

Your level of comfort with the inclusion of students on the spectrum through every facet of your programs will be reflected in the energy that comes back to you from teachers, staff members, parents, and other students. In this capacity, you are leading a movement: You are steering your entire community toward inclusivity. Your words and actions play a powerful role in the way people think and feel about students with autism in the classrooms.

Build Inclusive Familiarity and Fluency

Urge teachers and librarians to fill their shelves with material that focuses on the value and humanity of people who are different. For example, *Different Like Me: My*

Book of Autism Heroes by Jennifer Elder (2005), offers brief biographies of influential people who showed signs of ASD, including Hans Christian Andersen, Lewis Carroll, Albert Einstein, and Thomas Edison.

Suggest biographies of people who exemplify courage in the face of discrimination, such as Susan B. Anthony, Ruby Bridges, César Chávez, Anne Frank, Billie Jean King, Jackie Robinson, and Malala Yousefzai. Include biographies of individuals who have triumphed over physical challenges, such as Bethany Hamilton, Helen Keller, Franklin Delano Roosevelt, and Stevie Wonder.

Encourage teachers to choose or assign fictional books for class reading that explore adversity and resilience. Compelling examples include picture books like *Red: A Crayon's Story* by Michael Hall, which is about feeling different inside, and *Chrysanthemum* by Kevin Henkes, which features a spunky individualist; middle-grade novels like *Wonder* by R. J. Palacio, which depicts a determined protagonist who has a facial deformity, and *Out of My Mind* by Sharon Draper, narrated by a brilliant protagonist who has cerebral palsy; and teen and young adult novels like *See You at Harry's* by Jo Knowles, which addresses sexual orientation and grief, and *The Hate U Give* by Angie Thomas, which explores a teen's struggle with race and identity.

These are not heavy-handed, be-kind-to-your-classmate-with-autism books. They are just wonderful books that celebrate diversity and differences. (Visit http://barbaraboroson.com for a list of recommended children's books, organized by theme and reading level, all of which send quiet but powerful messages of inclusivity and acceptance.)

Implement Social-Emotional Learning

In addition to establishing and actively maintaining a cultural expectation of acceptance and inclusion, a great way to make an education community supportive of all students in terms of socialization and communication is by implementing an evidence-based social-emotional learning (SEL) program in your school or district. SEL is gaining in popularity throughout the United States, and it's familiar to many educators, but it also happens to dovetail beautifully with many of the priorities that have been addressed in this chapter for students on the spectrum.

The Collaborative for Academic, Social, and Emotional Learning (CASEL) defines SEL as "the process through which children and adults understand and manage emotions, set and achieve positive goals, feel and show empathy for others, establish and maintain positive relationships, and make responsible decisions" (CASEL, 2018, p. 1).

Setting an Inclusive Tone: The "Value Added" Perspective

Because students on the spectrum may at times appear quite loudly or flagrantly reactive, it's easy for their typical peers to dismiss them as a nuisance or an interruption and overlook their more subtle positive qualities. An important goal for inclusive schools is for typical students to learn to value their peers on the spectrum—to see and appreciate them and all that they bring to the community to make it richer and more interesting. It's up to you, their teachers, and the other adults in the school to set that tone.

Throughout high school, my son supplied jokes to the assistant principal to include in the morning announcements. Almost every morning, the assistant principal would explain over the loudspeaker, "Today's joke comes to you from our resident comedian" and then credit my son by name. My son became known around the school as the resident comedian—a point of pride for him, to be sure.

Diligently seek out meaningful ways to publicly acknowledge students on the spectrum, while taking care to not be cloying about it. Encourage teachers to look closely at each of their students on the spectrum and find *real* strengths that can be called out to demonstrate to the entire school community that these students not only belong but have something to contribute—even if this is just being their unique and quirky selves.

Let's take a look at some of the guiding tenets of effective SEL-based classrooms (Yoder & Gurke, 2017). Consider these in the context of their application to students on the spectrum, and you'll see how many of the concepts and suggestions provided previously in this chapter specifically for those students are now built into the SEL construct and being taught to everyone.

- Explicit lessons about social and emotional skills are taught, and those skills are integrated and reinforced throughout all other activities and content-area instruction.
- Student input is solicited and considered in the creation of classroom rules.
- Strategies are provided to help students monitor and regulate their behavior and emotions.
- Connections between effort and outcomes and between choices and consequences are made explicit for students in an effort to help them to learn to take responsibility for their actions.
- The classroom is structured so that all students feel included, appreciated, and safe to challenge themselves and make mistakes.
- Learning experiences reinforce positive social skills by encouraging peer collaboration, giving and receiving feedback, and working through difficulties and differences of opinion.
- Students take responsibility for their successes and their failures. The teacher supports students socially and emotionally while challenging them to achieve and surpass their goals.

Gehlbach (2017) notes that "at the core of SEL—after one peels away the surrounding layers—lies a single, teachable capacity that anchors almost all of our social interactions: *social perspective taking,* or the capacity to make sense of others' thoughts and feelings" (p. 9). In a sense, this is what inclusion is all about: creating a culture in which *all* students respect and learn from each other. This sets them up to be not only more successful and considerate learners in school, but also more effective and ethical citizens of the world.

● ▲ ◆ ◂ ■

It is imperative that we provide our students on the spectrum an environment in which they feel safe and socially accepted. But, as critical as that is, it's not enough to set them up for learning curricular content. For that, we need to dig deeper. In the next chapter, we will look at ways to reach students where they are and draw them out toward cognitive engagement.

Engagement and Content Acquisition

Teachers often find that even their most dynamic, inviting lesson plans and instructional strategies can fail to engage students on the spectrum. More frustrating still, even when teachers do manage to capture the elusive attention of a student on the spectrum, the information they teach doesn't seem to stick. In this chapter, we'll take a look at challenges of engagement and content acquisition and at ways you can support your teachers' efforts to both reach and teach their students on the spectrum.

Decoding Engagement and Content Acquisition

Anxiety, sensory, and social distress would be enough to interfere with anyone's readiness for learning. But even when we are able to ease those challenges for our students on the spectrum, other challenges related to acquiring and processing information obstruct their ability to engage in content and to assimilate it effectively.

Engagement Challenges

Before content instruction can even begin, students on the spectrum need to feel safe and calm in the classroom. This requires faithful adherence to visual schedules, a sensitively modulated sensory environment, and a learning space that is welcoming, supportive, and bully-proof. But even then, obstacles to academic engagement for students on the spectrum are plentiful. Let's consider the most intrusive challenges in terms of the ways they affect engagement: *socialization, perseveration,* and *eye contact.*

Socialization and Engagement

Some of the social challenges discussed in Chapter 5 also interfere with classroom engagement.

Joint attention. Difficulties with joint attention can obstruct students' innate motivation or interest in the curriculum and get in the way of a growth mindset.

Mindblindness. Mindblindness can prevent these students from recognizing what is important to the teachers and, therefore, what is important for them to attend to. They may zero in on aspects of the instruction or curriculum that are incidental rather than critical, or that are relevant to their interests but not salient to the teachers' instructional objective.

Perseveration and Engagement

As discussed in previous chapters, students on the autism spectrum tend to be immersed in their own thoughts. Perhaps they retreat into their solitary comfort zones because the big wide world feels overwhelming. Or perhaps the big wide world feels overwhelming because they are so caught up in their solitary comfort zones. Regardless of which is the chicken and which the egg, students on the spectrum need support opening up to the world around them: engaging in it and learning from it.

When students on the autism spectrum are highly preoccupied or immersed in very circumscribed areas of interest, this is called *perseveration*. Perseverative interests can range from everyday topics, such as buses, trains, and movies, to more unlikely topics, such as airplane engines, ceiling fans, dinosaurs, and many others. Why do these become perseverative topics for students on the autism spectrum? Presumably because the predictability of these topics makes them appealing in their reliability. Buses and trains come and go according to a fixed schedule and follow prescribed routes. A movie is exactly, blissfully the same every time it's watched. Engines and other mechanical objects operate in programmed and prescribed ways. Ceiling fans go around and around and around and never deviate. Dinosaurs are extinct; students can count on the fact that there's not much unexpected change happening in the world of dinosaurs.

As we know, students on the spectrum feel safer focusing on their perseverative areas of interest than risking engagement in the unpredictable social world that swirls around them. By the same token, staying focused on those perseverative areas of interest also feels safer than risking engagement in the new and unfamiliar curricular content that teachers present. The problem here is that curricular content is almost always *new* to students—in fact, that's the very reason it's being taught! So just when teachers need students to be at their most open and receptive, students on the spectrum are most likely to shut down and retreat. They withdraw to their comfort zones, to what they know, to what doesn't change. Because of this, perseveration persistently thwarts teachers' ability to draw students on the spectrum toward engaging in academic content.

Eye Contact and Engagement

Sometimes it can be hard to tell whether students on the spectrum are engaged or not. This is partly due to their difficulties with making eye contact. Eye contact is commonly perceived by adults as a necessary signifier of attention and respect. The absence of it suggests to us that students are disengaged, distracted, and discourteous. Therefore, adults often demand eye contact. While it is fine to encourage it, we should never require it. Here's why.

Given the many challenges we have discussed to this point, you are surely aware that baseline anxiety among students on the spectrum is generally high, especially in inclusion classrooms. These students are working much harder than their typical peers just to sit still, listen, stay engaged, process information, and make relevant associations. As if that's not enough, at the same time, they are exerting conscious energy to resist instinctive behaviors like calling out, flapping their hands, humming, and contemplating the exoskeleton of their favorite arthropod. At best that may be about all they can handle at one time. Making eye contact may be one task too many.

Eye contact with students on the spectrum can be fleeting at best and may be limited for several reasons (see Figure 6.1).

Content Acquisition Challenges

In addition to engagement challenges, teachers bump up against content acquisition challenges that interfere with the ability of students on the spectrum to assimilate information in productive, meaningful, and retrievable ways. These include the challenges of *language and communication, concrete thinking, cognitive processing,* and *generalization.*

Figure 6.1: Obstacles to Eye Contact for Students on the Autism Spectrum

Area of Challenge	Obstacles
Sensation	• Direct eye contact may feel too intense and may cause sensory overload or even pain. • Eye contact can be disconcerting because the eyes of others are constantly shifting and darting around. • The movement of lashes as other people blink may be distracting, as it can make eyes seem to flash and flicker.
Motor Control	• Some students do not have the ocular-motor control necessary to stabilize their eyes. They may be unable to hold their eyes steady enough to maintain eye contact. • Some students may have difficulty directing their eyes to focus on a specific target, such as another person's eyes. • Students with ocular-motor challenges may not be able to follow the movements of other people's eyes across the midline. (They may also struggle to track words across a page while reading or follow an object that moves across the center of their field of vision.)
Social Communication	• Direct eye contact can cause intense social anxiety. • Some students on the spectrum may not perceive the value of eye contact as a component of communication. They are likely to overlook messages being sent through someone's eyes. • Students on the spectrum may also fail to consider the messages they are sending with their own eye contact or lack thereof.

Language, Communication, and Content Acquisition

Issues related to language and communication, discussed in Chapter 5, affect not only socialization but also content acquisition.

Receptive language. Difficulties with receptive language can interfere with students' ability to process and comprehend instructions and curricular content. This can make them unable to comply with directives or process information in ways that meet teachers' expectations.

Nonverbal and paraverbal communication. Difficulties with nonverbal and paraverbal communication can cause students to miss key elements of teachers' instructions that may be expressed through subtext and body language. A large portion of intended meaning is encoded in nonverbal and paraverbal communication, so significant information may be misinterpreted or entirely overlooked by students on the spectrum.

Concrete Thinking and Content Acquisition

The fact that students on the spectrum tend to be primarily concrete thinkers (as discussed in Chapter 5) can impede not only their social skills but also their ability to fully comprehend curricular content, especially in the upper elementary grades and beyond. While their typical peers have advanced to the level of "reading to learn" and have begun to explore symbolic, analytical, metaphorical, philosophical, and meta-cognitive concepts, students on the spectrum may remain quite limited in the depth of their understanding.

Concrete thinking, along with cognitive processing challenges, can also make it difficult for these students to assimilate individual concepts into a broader context or a meaningful whole and can limit their ability to generalize ideas.

Cognitive Processing and Content Acquisition

Central coherence theory is one way that scientists explain how information is processed in the human brain. As explained by the American Psychological Association in the *APA Dictionary of Psychology* (2015), central coherence theory holds that, by and large,

> human beings have an inherent drive to form coherent wholes by integrating pieces of relevant information. Most people tend to process incoming stimuli in context in order to derive a meaningful gist of the situation, often at the expense of surface details. By contrast, individuals with autism spectrum disorder exhibit a tendency toward weak central coherence, which results in an over-reliance on local or piecemeal processing and a failure to integrate information in order to process stimuli in context. (p. 168)

Central coherence can be broken down into two prevailing components: *global coherence* and *local coherence*. Individuals who have strong global coherence would be able to look at an expansive cluster of trees and see a forest; individuals who have strong local coherence would look at an expansive cluster of trees and see, well, an expansive cluster of trees.

When operating in a typical fashion, strong central coherence compels us to prioritize the understanding of meaning and to make sense of our perceptions by noting or creating connections and meaningful links, even among disparate elements. Uta Frith (1989), professor emeritus at the Institute of Cognitive Neuroscience at the University College London and the originator of the concept of central coherence, posited that in children with autism, the capacity for global coherence is diminished. For them, individual or local ideas and thoughts tend to be detached from context and lack meaningful connectedness with one another.

Frith and her colleague Francesca Happé describe someone with strong local coherence as being able to identify the melodic pitch of the sound a cork makes as it pops out of a bottle or identify a dozen brands of vacuum cleaner by their sound alone (Happé & Frith, 2006). At times, this highly circumscribed focus can lead to stunning discoveries that would not be possible if an individual were distracted by bigger-picture concepts. But the limitations of local coherence leave a lot of kids lost in the forest.

Students who have strong local coherence (at the expense of strong global coherence) would struggle to ascertain which elements of a concept are the more salient (and therefore the most important to retain) and which might be considered to be subsidiary or background information. Today's challenging academic learning standards demand strong global coherence. For example, English language arts standards require critical thinking, getting the gist or main idea, summarizing, recognizing broad themes, comparing and contrasting concepts, creating core concepts, and supporting ideas with evidence. Math standards require students to contextualize and decontextualize algorithms, recognize and utilize repeated reasoning, evaluate equivalencies and proportions, and understand the essential variability of variables. These skills and others depend on strong global coherence.

Strong local coherence and diminished global coherence affect cognitive organization, too. When it comes to assimilating information, individual ideas and concepts get cognitively filed in discrete bits and are not placed into meaningful context. That makes them very difficult to retrieve when needed.

Imagine the brain as a filing cabinet. When neurotypical thinkers acquire new information, we unconsciously make associations. We place the new information into a relevant context and file it into a specific folder that contains thematically related information. Then, whenever we need to retrieve it, we know exactly where to find it and can access it readily.

For many students on the spectrum, it's as though they have no folders in their cognitive filing cabinet. When new ideas and bits of information arrive, they get chucked into a drawer and are not filed or placed in relation to other relevant information. The drawer fills up with other isolated chunks of information, and so when these students need to retrieve a specific idea, they can't find it; it's in there *somewhere,* but they can't quite get a hold of it.

This is why teachers and parents of these students often find that information a student seemed to understand just yesterday seems to be gone today, or that information they've taught dozens of times seems still to be unfamiliar. You, too, are likely to face a situation in which you debrief a behavioral issue with a student one day and feel you really got through—and then the same problematic behavior is repeated the very next day. One explanation for this may be that the student was preoccupied with perseverating while being taught the new concept and never took in the information at all. Another possible explanation is that the information was, in fact, received and filed but is now irretrievable. In other situations, the problem may be one of inadequate generalization.

Generalization and Content Acquisition

Concrete thinking also compromises students' ability to understand how much to generalize information. Usually, the extent to which information should be generalized is intuitive. But, as discussed in Chapter 5, if we want students on the spectrum to learn something, we need to spell it out in explicit detail and not leave it to intuition. Indeed, every lesson must be made explicit—even generalization.

Overgeneralizing. Sometimes students on the spectrum overgeneralize information. Here's an example. Brianna, a student I worked with, liked to hug her classmates—an overzealous greeting her 5th grade peers did not generally appreciate. Brianna's teachers taught her that a high five would be a more welcome greeting. Agreeably, Brianna began high-fiving her peers instead of hugging them, but, knowing that this new greeting style was teacher-sanctioned, she did it repeatedly throughout the school day, every single time she encountered a classmate. This amounted to dozens of high fives per classmate per day, and Brianna's behavior began to cause her peers' patience—as well as their palms—to chafe. Relief came when Brianna's teacher added the specific and explicit detail that a high five is an appropriate greeting *only the first time you see a classmate each day*. After that, Brianna had not only a new skill but also clear parameters for its generalization, and she complied readily.

Undergeneralizing. As much as overgeneralizing is a problem for students on the spectrum, undergeneralizing is even more common. At one elementary school where I consulted, Ian, a 1st grader, was working hard on meeting his handwriting goal in occupational therapy (OT). One day, his occupational therapist announced to Ian's classroom teacher that Ian had achieved his handwriting goal. How exciting! But Ian's teacher was dumbfounded. As far as she had seen, Ian had demonstrated no improvement in handwriting at all.

The two educators compared notebooks and saw that Ian was using completely different handwriting in OT than he was in the classroom and on his homework. Together, they asked Ian why he wasn't using his beautiful new handwriting in the classroom and at home. Ian shrugged. He had no idea. It had simply not occurred to him to do that. He knew that his new handwriting was pleasing his occupational therapist, so he had continued using it in OT, but what did that have to do with anyone or anywhere else?

Ian's teacher and therapist congratulated him again on having developed such lovely new handwriting and then instructed him explicitly that he was now expected to use that new handwriting *everywhere, all the time*. Ian shrugged again and went on to do exactly that—because he had been told to.

Although Ian was willing and able to comply with generalizing his new skill across contexts once he had been specifically told to do so, the idea that he should generalize this skill had not occurred to him on his own. One reason many students on the autism spectrum undergeneralize information is their failure to attribute intrinsic value to certain skills and abilities. In this example, Ian hadn't perceived any inherent value in neat handwriting over messy handwriting. A typical student of his age would recognize and take pride in the value factor of the different styles of handwriting and would naturally integrate the new skills into the old, eventually supplanting the old handwriting with the new-and-improved version. Ian was missing the broader context—the *why,* which is yet another component of the hidden curriculum.

Rule following. Temple Grandin (2008), a world-renowned inventor and professor of animal science who is on the autism spectrum, explains that she still struggles to generalize rules. Even as an accomplished adult, she grapples with the confusing parameters of rules and the *unruly* fact that rules themselves do not follow predictable rules: Some rules are absolute, and some can be manipulated within reason. Other rules seem to lurk in the hidden curriculum—expected to be followed, but never taught or stated. Grandin has created for herself some *rules for rules* by sorting rules into categories. Let's look at how complicated rule following is when generalization is a challenge.

Rules for illegal and unacceptable actions. These are the rules that mustn't ever be broken—rules that prohibit killing or stealing, for example. At school, certain rules cover actions that are never, ever acceptable. These are the relatively easy ones for students on the spectrum to follow because they are inviolable: No starting a fire. No bringing a gun to school, no smoking in school, and so on.

Rules for illegal but "acceptable" actions. These are rules that people often break even though doing so is against the law. For example, driving over the speed limit and littering are, in fact, against the law, but many people still speed and litter and rarely get in trouble. The application and interpretation of these laws are fluid, which makes them tricky for anyone prone to overgeneralization to understand.

At school, it's against the rules for students to use their phones during class, but students often type away under their desks and rarely get in trouble. It's against the rules to curse at school, but students do it all the time out of earshot of adults. Rules like these are especially problematic because many students on the spectrum find it necessary to correct their peers when they push those permeable boundaries.

Rules of courtesy. These are rules that are not laws and are OK to break—but only sometimes. For example, it's a rule to not tell lies. But in certain circumstances, lying is not only encouraged but expected. These include showing appreciation for an unwanted gift (e.g., *Thank you. I love it*) or complimenting an unfortunate style choice (e.g., *Oh, yes! You look great*).

At school, it's against the rules for students to "copy" one another's work, but it's considered courteous to let someone who missed class copy your notes. Similarly, students are taught that when they see a peer doing something wrong and tell on her strictly for the purpose of getting her in trouble (*Ella isn't paying attention!*), it's called "tattling," and it's not acceptable. But if they see a peer doing something wrong and tell on her for the purpose of getting someone else *out of* trouble (*Ella is bothering Simon!*), it's called "reporting" and it's not only acceptable—it's encouraged.

Rules in the hidden curriculum. These rules address behaviors that are expected even though there are no stated rules addressing them. These unspoken rules, often thought of as "common sense," include stepping out of the way when someone wants to get by, not pulling on someone's arm when they're holding a cup of hot coffee, or not texting someone 20 times if they haven't texted you back.

At school, unstated rules might include not eating food out of someone else's lunchbox, not shimmying up the flagpole, not throwing paper clips out the window, and countless others. These are expectations no one thinks to make explicit . . . until we find we need to.

Leading the Way to Successful Inclusion

The challenges described in this chapter are all significant barriers to effective academic learning. In order to teach these students content, we first need to reach them. And that takes a whole lot of patience and a little bit of ingenuity.

Explaining the Why

Contextualizing content is good practice in general, of course, but for students on the spectrum, it's essential. Because these students struggle to contextualize information on their own, it's up to educators to create and label the cognitive file folders so students will know exactly where to place the new information and will be able to retrieve it and apply it precisely as needed. These students need to know how the new information connects with what's already been covered and why adding it is important. For teachers, this means explaining *why* they are teaching what they are teaching. Ian needs to know *why* he is working on his handwriting.

Here's an example of a contextualizing statement a high school English teacher might use at the beginning of a lesson:

> *Now I want to tell you a bit about the Russian Revolution. What possible reasons can you think of to explain why, here in English class, in the middle of reading* Animal Farm, *we are suddenly going to talk about the Russian Revolution?*

A guided class discussion about why this connection is being made will place the lesson in context. The same teacher might wrap up the lesson by reiterating its connection to the content:

Now you know a bit about the Russian Revolution. As we continue to read Animal Farm, *please jot down anything you notice that might pertain not only to the farm but also to the Russian Revolution. Think about why the author is drawing this connection. What does he want us to think about?*

Again, these kinds of prompts and explicit expectations help all students—not just those on the spectrum—to build connections between otherwise discrete topics. They encourage students to note the interrelatedness of many aspects of the curriculum and add them together, constructing and developing a whole that is greater than the sum of its parts. This is how they get the big picture.

While *Animal Farm*'s connection to the Russian Revolution is a very high-level example, all teachers can support this kind of holistic, fluid thinking by supplying all students with graphic organizers that guide them to consider content in relation to other content. Helpful concept organizers for students on the spectrum include timelines, character trees, storyboards, sequencing grids, Venn diagrams, cluster maps, concept webs, compare-and-contrast charts, sketch-noting templates, and more. The explicit relational placement of new topics with more familiar topics is an important visual and concrete means for helping students understand the big picture.

Providing Parameters of Generalization

Students on the spectrum also need help with big-picture thinking and generalization in social and behavioral contexts. As mentioned previously, these students far prefer to follow rules than to break them. If you have students on the spectrum who are off task or breaking rules, it is most likely because they don't understand those rules or don't understand the terms of generalization—not that they are being willful or oppositional. When the PE teacher comes knocking at your door, complaining that Miko refuses to run the bases in the gym, do some reconnaissance to figure out why. Perhaps she had been taught the rule "No running indoors" and was following that rule to the letter. In your effort to make sure that your rules are indisputably clear and accurately implemented, be sure to include the terms of generalization along with any instruction—in this case: *"No running indoors, except in the gym."*

Students on the spectrum would be most comfortable (and best able to be compliant) if all of these rules were explicitly stated, explained, checked for understanding, and then applied and interpreted with utter consistency. But that's just not the way it goes. And this makes life extremely confusing and challenging for these students who really crave clear and consistent rules to guide their functioning. As an education leader, it is critical that you understand and recognize the cognitive dissonance this creates for these students. They want more than anything to comply. They think they are, in fact, complying. But they keep getting it wrong.

Give students on the spectrum the benefit of the doubt that when they break important rules, it's due to confusion. When you are presented with students on the spectrum who have broken rules, make it your first move to investigate and address the following questions:

- What is this student's specific understanding of the rule?
- Was the rule ever explicitly taught, or was it just presumed?
- If the rule was taught, which kind of rule is it (e.g., a rule for an illegal but accepted action, a rule of courtesy, a rule in the hidden curriculum)?
- How consistent is this rule's interpretation and application?
- Have the terms of generalization been explained?

Do everything you can to gently teach or reteach, always checking for understanding. Set the terms of generalization. Talk about acceptable exceptions to the rule. And remind your teachers to do the same.

Here is an example of debriefing, setting a new rule, and including its terms of generalization. At the end of an intense winter, my driveway was covered with a two-inch layer of solid ice. I got my then-teenaged son to go outside with me so we could chop up that ice. We were side by side, chopping away, when all of a sudden, I slipped. I went down hard, landing on my hip and on the heel of my hand. I know I made an awful sound on the way down and an even worse sound when I hit the ice. My son was only a few feet away. He saw and heard the whole thing. But did he come rushing over to help me up? Did he exclaim, "Oh my gosh, Mom! Are you OK?" Nope. Instead, as I lay in pain on the ice, he said, "Hey! Can you do that again, so I can record it?"

I will freely admit that I was not in a "teachable moment" place just then.

A couple of hours later, my son and I sat down together to debrief the situation. As soon as I explained to him that the fall had hurt my body and that his words had hurt my feelings, he felt awful about it. He jumped up, gave me a hug, and ran to the kitchen to get me an icepack. It was a perfect empathic response . . . aside from coming two hours after the fact.

But the most important component of debriefing is always ensuring that new behavioral actions and reactions are learned and assimilated. "Listen," I said to my son. "The next time this happens, you need to offer help."

That's pretty clear, right? Well, no, because I hadn't included any terms of generalization. As soon as the words were out of my mouth, I knew my son would undergeneralize it. He would offer help the *next time* (not any other time) that *I* (and only I) slipped and fell *on ice* (and only ice) that was *in our driveway* (and nowhere else). However, should someone who's not me slip and fall . . . on grease or on a banana peel, in a garage or on a sidewalk or anywhere else near my son, at any other time in the future . . . all bets would be off.

So I revised my instruction to include the explicit parameters of generalization: "Actually, here's what has to happen: *any* time you see *any*one fall, *any*where, for *any* reason, for the *rest of your life,* you need to offer help." And now he's got it.

Sure, someday he may overgeneralize that instruction and rush to help someone who flops down playfully on a trampoline, but in this case, better to overgeneralize than to undergeneralize.

Getting Students Engaged in Content

Perseveration can make it extremely difficult for students on the spectrum to be "available" to learn any kinds of lessons. In this way, it may be seen as a barrier to learning. But trying to wrench perseverative students out of their comfort zone is a surefire way to upend their hard-won equilibrium and trigger a shutdown or an emotional or behavioral outburst. So how can we reach these students? Rather than try to push through perseveration, educators will have better success working from the inside out: meeting these students where they are and gently drawing them out to a more open and receptive place where they are ready to learn.

In this section we will look at ways to use perseveration as a way *in*. This means joining them in their safe space and then gently broadening and expanding their focus so that the new material feels familiar and, therefore, safe. I call this *finding the hook,* and it's about using a student's special interest to lure them into considering a new topic. Whether a student is preoccupied with insects, hurricanes, rocket propulsion, the line of ascension to the British throne, Disney movies, or anything else, there is always a way to link a student's special interest to the curriculum—at any level.

Depending on the student's topic of interest and the teacher's intended lesson, finding the hook can be quite simple or might require just a quick bit of preliminary research. In one high school biology inclusion classroom where I consulted, the curricular unit was human anatomy. Jian, a student on the spectrum, was not interested in learning about anatomy. He was interested only in clocks and watches. He was fixated on the differences between digital and analog, he monitored closely the movement of the second hand on the wall clock, and he asked everyone who wore a watch about its make and model. The teachers in the classroom could not get Jian to focus on their lesson.

When I suggested that we *use* Jian's interest in clocks and watches to lead him toward anatomy, the teachers were not only skeptical but also resistant. It was all they could do to get Jian to stop thinking and talking about his preoccupation. Now I was asking them to bring it into the curriculum? I assured them that it would be a very temporary measure and a worthwhile investment in actually moving Jian away from clocks and watches. I proposed that we work with Jian to take apart an old clock.

The next day I brought in an old analog clock, and while the other students in the class studied a human skeleton, Jian performed an eager, amateur autopsy on the clock. We talked about its parts in terms of anatomy so that he would become familiar with the concepts of anatomy in the context of the clock. I referred to the metal components as the "bones" of the clock. We talked about the battery as though it were the heart of the clock—the battery kept the clock running, until it ran out of energy. We examined the gears, which I compared to human joints. We talked about how, like people, clocks may look very different from one another on the outside but have inner mechanisms that are quite similar. Jian was engaged throughout the clock autopsy, and in the process, he inadvertently learned a bit about anatomy: bones, joints, and hearts. The connections I made for him were loose—certainly not scientific. But that didn't really matter. Jian was engaged, and I was hooking him into the concept of anatomy.

After that, when the teachers tried again to teach Jian about human anatomy, the topic sounded a little familiar to him, a little safer, because it felt to Jian like it had something to do with clocks. They framed it explicitly in a way that would intrigue him: "Remember when you learned all about the anatomy of a clock? Well, humans have bones and joints, too, just like a clock does. Let's take a look."

Going Deeper

Sometimes a student will perseverate on a topic that is unfamiliar to the teachers. In that case, just a bit of research is all that's needed. At one elementary school where I consulted, a student's topic of perseverative interest was the TV series *SpongeBob SquarePants,* which was only vaguely familiar to me at the time. A quick Google search of *SpongeBob* episodes yielded a vast array of themes: pineapples, fast food, sea life, camping, labor strikes, roller coasters, and many others that can be creatively linked to the curriculum (see Figure 6.2).

Tapping into students' interests in order to engage them in a lesson or activity is a familiar page in most teachers' playbooks. When doing so with the perseverative interests of students on the spectrum, the aim is to move away from the perseveration as quickly as possible. Once they've considered, for example, how labor laws relate to *SpongeBob,* they are likely to be more open to learning (along with the rest of the class) about the history of the treatment of workers around the word, the Triangle Shirtwaist Factory fire, the emergence of labor unions, the U.S. immigrant experience in the early 1900s, and a host of other similar topics.

Try to let teachers know that you understand that their lessons may veer off in unexpected directions. They can't know exactly what perseverative topics their students on the spectrum will inject into their classroom, but they need to be ready to run with anything. I chose *SpongeBob* for this hypothetical example not because I'm a fan—fact is, I'm not!—but to demonstrate that a hook can be found fairly easily to connect all sorts of perseveration to the curriculum. The teachers you lead can learn to link any curricular content to any perseverative interest a student might have—even to topics with which the teachers are unfamiliar.

Figure 6.2: Finding the Hook: Engagement Opportunities Through
SpongeBob SquarePants

Content Area	Thematic Connection	Possible Student Activities	Next Steps
Math	Look for the presence of numbers in *SpongeBob* (e.g., on the menu of his favorite restaurant, The Krusty Krab), and use them to teach math skills. Then expand by seguing into higher-level calculations, algorithms, etc.	• Calculate the cost of a meal or of multiple meals at The Krusty Krab. • Divide the cost per character of a shared tab at The Krusty Krab, or calculate what percent of the total bill was spent by each character. • Solve for items that were ordered at The Krusty Krab but didn't show up at the table.	• Segue into skill building with addition. • Segue into skill building with division, fractions, and percentages. • Segue to unknowns, variables, and algebra.
English language arts	Use *SpongeBob* as a thematic jumping-off point for writing, reading, spelling, and grammar. Then expand by segueing into elements of setting, characterization, literary devices, story arcs, etc.	• Write a fantasy about an underwater adventure with SpongeBob. • Consider what's wrong with the spelling of "The Krusty Krab." • Read *SpongeBob* books (it's not exactly classic literature, but it is a place to start!).	• Segue to writing adventure stories on other topics to support skill building. • Segue to studying alliteration and other literary devices. • Segue to reading fiction on related topics, like *20,000 Leagues Under the Sea* or *Magic Tree House: Dark Day in the Deep Sea*. Expand to other Magic Tree House books that lead readers on dozens of other adventures.

Content Area	Thematic Connection	Possible Student Activities	Next Steps
Science	Look for adventures that SpongeBob and his friends have that relate to science. Discuss those connections and then expand by going deeper into related elements of biology, earth science, chemistry, physics, etc.	• Explore the marine life that SpongeBob encounters in his underwater community. • Research the composition of SpongeBob's home on the ocean floor. • Examine the variable speed and velocity of SpongeBob's dreaded rollercoaster ride.	• Segue to studying environmental issues that affect marine life and then environmental issues that affect humans. • Segue to studying the composition of sea water, the layers of Earth's crust, and Earth's atmosphere. • Segue to studying the physics of energy and momentum.
Social studies	Consider *SpongeBob* from a sociological and anthropological perspective. Discuss the show as if it represents a society. Then expand to topical lessons related to social structure, economics, government, etc.	• Examine the social strata in SpongeBob's hometown of Bikini Bottom. • Consider whether SpongeBob's underwater community could be considered a civilization. • Investigate the labor laws that might have protected SpongeBob when he walked off his job.	• Segue to studying income inequality or caste systems. • Segue to discussion of ancient civilizations and the development of modern civilization. • Segue to discussion of the development of labor unions, the Triangle Shirtwaist Factory Fire, and immigration.

Note: This table is available for download from http://barbaraboroson.com/FindingTheHook.pdf.

So when you pop into classrooms, don't be surprised to find the students immersed in underwater fantasies or the curriculum saturated by fast-food facts and other obscure and wildly extracurricular investigations. It's all part of the journey toward engagement.

Setting an Inclusive Tone: Looking Back and Moving Forward

Without doubt, including students on the autism spectrum in general education settings makes teaching harder. Even inclusion teachers who embrace the challenge and differentiate their curriculum and activities in new directions have their work cut out for them.

Because students on the spectrum have difficulty assimilating, retrieving, and generalizing information, learning can be excruciatingly slow and often imperceptible. Although it may be possible to see progress in the rearview mirror, on a day-to-day basis, it's easy for teachers to feel discouraged or hopeless.

Remind teachers that even when it feels like a student is taking three steps forward and two steps back, that's still forward movement. Since teachers are deep in the weeds with these students, help them see the light of day by pointing out a student's progress in other areas or positive changes you have noticed in that student since the school year began. (Read about measuring progress in Chapter 7.) Teachers can feel renewed when they are reminded to take a look back at where a student started and at how far they've actually traveled together. Acknowledging the extra effort these teachers are putting in can go a long way toward helping them feel effective and stay energized and hopeful.

Eye Contact Optional

Most students on the spectrum are actually better able to engage in a lesson or a conversation *without* the added strain of having to make eye contact. Fortunately, there are ways other than eye contact that students on the autism spectrum can demonstrate that they are listening and absorbing information:

- To demonstrate attention, students can be encouraged to look at your face, without having to look directly at your eyes.
- To demonstrate engagement, students can be directed to look at the screen where information is being presented or at the activity, rather than at your eyes.

- To demonstrate comprehension, students can be asked to repeat back information or content, putting it into their own words. If they can't speak or they struggle to articulate their understanding, they can write or type out what's been said in their own words, or they can draw a picture illustrating the meaning.

- To demonstrate respect, students can be reminded to use respectful words when speaking to adults. And adults can be reminded to accept these alternative presentations as absolutely adequate substitutes for eye contact in this context.

Connecting with students on the spectrum requires us all to step just a little bit off our well-worn paths to meet them where they are. Thankfully, there's a map for that: universal design for learning.

Universal Design for Learning

Universal design for learning (UDL) is an educational framework that guides the development and design of flexible, multilevel learning experiences—exactly the kind of differentiated approach that is needed for students on the spectrum. A curriculum informed by UDL is designed with the expectation that it will be used by students who have diverse skills and abilities; it's built for differentiation, allowing for universal application.

The tenets of UDL empower educators to meet students' diverse needs through the implementation of flexible instructional materials, techniques, and strategies. Given the universal nature of their application, these strategies fit neatly under the umbrella of MTSS (multitiered systems of support). A universally designed curriculum is formulated to meet the needs of the greatest number of users—that is, an MTSS Tier 1 intervention—effectively eliminating later-stage modifications and adaptations that are costly not only to your programs but also to the quality of the education of the students who need them.

The prevailing intent of UDL is to fix the curriculum to fit the students rather than try to fix the students to fit the curriculum. As explained by the nonprofit education research organization CAST (2018), UDL guides three main principles of instruction: representation, action and expression, and engagement. Any school that includes students who function in ways that don't quite fit into prefab learning categories (read: *every* school) should be familiar with these principles and taking steps put them into practice. Let's look a little more closely at each.

Principle 1: Representation

UDL's principle of representation directs teachers to utilize multiple means of presenting content. This is the "what" of learning—information, concepts, and ideas. UDL encourages representation of content at varied levels of complexity. For example, instead of assigning only one science textbook to everyone in the class, teachers can provide alternative reading materials that describe similar ideas at higher levels for high-performing readers and at simpler levels or in more interactive ways for students who are struggling readers or learners.

As previously discussed, students on the spectrum tend to understand information best when it is presented in concrete terms with visual aids, explicitly linked to personal areas of high interest, and positioned conceptually in relation to prior knowledge. UDL suggests various routes to this kind of supportive, challenging, well-differentiated instruction. Tools and techniques to consider include recorded books, online or video presentations, interactive learning stations, flipped classroom arrangements, and assorted graphic organizers, among many other creative approaches.

Principle 2: Action and Expression

UDL's principle of action and expression acknowledges the challenges of executive function and communication by allowing for numerous means of acquiring information and demonstrating knowledge—the "how" of learning. Given that areas of strength and challenge can be highly variable among students on the spectrum, these students benefit from having options for acquiring and expressing information. Because their skills can be so splintered, it's particularly important that teachers find ways, for example, to explore comprehension without requiring that every student read aloud; to imbue historical knowledge without requiring memorization; and to accept mathematical solutions even when their computational processes cannot be shown.

Whenever possible, let all students have choices regarding how they demonstrate their knowledge. Provide options for writing, typing, singing, dancing, pantomiming, painting, sculpting, collaging, montaging, podcasting, creating slide presentations, or capturing video footage. Especially with students on the spectrum who have so many areas of challenge, options are a great way to let them capitalize on their strengths to show what they know.

Principle 3: Engagement

UDL's principle of engagement relates to stimulating interest and motivation for learning. Engagement is the "why" of learning. As CAST (2018) puts it:

> Information that is not attended to, that does not engage learners' cognition, is in fact inaccessible. It is inaccessible both in the moment and in the future, because relevant information goes unnoticed and unprocessed. . . . It is, therefore, important to have alternative ways to recruit learner interest, ways that reflect the important inter- and intra-individual differences amongst learners. (UDL Guideline 7)

Note how closely that sentiment aligns with this book's goals and strategies for meeting the specific needs of students on the spectrum. In accordance with the UDL engagement strategies already suggested in the previous section, the guidelines issued by CAST (2018) suggest that teachers try to do the following for *all students:*

- Optimize relevance by personalizing and contextualizing content to align with learners' personal lives (UDL Checkpoint 7.2).
- Minimize threats and distraction by creating a supportive classroom environment, diminishing risk, following routines, incorporating graphic organizers, reducing unexpected events, and modulating sensory stimulation (UDL Checkpoint 7.3).
- Provide options for self-regulation by prompts and guiding self-reflection and self-reinforcement (UDL Checkpoint 9.1)
- Facilitate personal coping skills and strategies by scaffolding frustration and emotional management skills and bolstering self-awareness. (UDL Checkpoint 9.2) .

● ⋏ ◆ ◀ ■

UDL aligns perfectly with the goals of engaging and teaching students on the spectrum alongside their typically developing peers. Advocating for a curriculum that is flexible enough to meet the needs of everyone empowers all to access the curriculum. No one way of learning is better or worse, greater than or less than; every way is different, just as every student is different on our diverse and inclusive educational frontier.

Those differences extend to behavior, too. In Chapter 7, we will look closely at challenging behavior in the context of students on the spectrum and at how best to respond.

Behavior

As described in the preceding chapters, the disruptive behaviors of students who are on the autism spectrum are usually triggered by unexpected change, loss of comfort anchors, dysregulation, sensory imbalance, social stress, communication obstacles, and learning challenges—all of which contribute to overwhelming anxiety. Students' responses to that anxiety and to those many frustrations are further compromised by executive dysfunction, which derails their best intentions to be flexible, cooperative, and calm.

If you and the educators you supervise have worked to preempt and address behavior challenges by adapting the environment and the curriculum, and by providing students with adaptive coping strategies, then you have already done a great deal to diminish students' stress. As a result, you have mitigated the likelihood that they will behave in ways that disrupt their own learning and that of their classmates. By taking these powerful preventive measures, you have headed off innumerable behavioral outbursts that could have had lasting effects on your students on the spectrum, their classmates, their teachers and supporters, and yourself. Take a moment to appreciate what you *haven't* had to deal with. That's huge.

However, it's not possible to preempt all challenging situations; difficult behavior *will* happen. And when it does, it tends to come knocking, banging, yelling, and kicking at your door. You need to be ready.

Decoding Disruptive Behavior and School Responses

When teachers send students to administrators for intervention, those teachers are at the end of their rope. They may be looking for their leaders to respond with consequences or another kind of disciplinary action.

As a leader, of course you want to be supportive of your teachers, to show them that you've got their back. But you are also responsible for running a program that is meaningfully inclusive, one that truly embraces and honors the diversity it represents. A large cohort in that diversity arrives on your doorstep in the form of the differently abled—students who need behavior interventions that are just as differentiated as their academic interventions.

Let's take a closer look at the behaviors of students on the spectrum and try to read between the lines. Decoding what's really going on when these students behave in distracting or disruptive ways is the necessary first step to responding in a manner that makes things better, not worse, and providing both the students and their teachers with the differentiated support they need.

Behavior as Communication

As explained in Chapter 5, all students on the spectrum struggle with communication. Whether the issues are related to speech, semantic language, pragmatic language, social reciprocity, or mindblindness, these challenges are ever-present and pushed to their limits in an inclusion classroom. When a student is under stress, those fragile skills run for cover.

My son, who is now a highly articulate and well-spoken young adult, loses access to his otherwise impressive vocabulary when he is anxious. In a stressful situation, words truly fail him. When the toilet got backed up recently, he ran to me, clearly agitated, and demanded, "Come! The thing happened! The thing!"

"What thing?" I asked, calmly.

"The thing! *It! You* know—*IT! It happened!*"

When language and coping skills fail them, students may react to troubling situations with behavior. Instinctive responses such as fight, flight, or freeze may kick in when any situation feels overwhelming to them, even if it seems benign to others. Here's a point that can't be stressed enough: For students on the spectrum, big responses and impulsive reactions are not choices. Nor are they overblown or melodramatic. Executive dysfunction derails efforts to stay calm, stop and think, reflect, predict—the coping skills many of us use subconsciously to avert panic. These students may go straight to panic.

Setting an Inclusive Tone: The Search for Meaning

Even when the actions and expressions of students are utterly incomprehensible to you, never assume that they are without meaning. Have the humility and generosity to refrain from dismissing students' words or actions as meaningless simply because you don't understand them. Instead, act on the assumption that meaning is *inherent*, even if it's not *apparent*. Take the time to dig a little deeper. You'll find it.

About Behavior Policies

Traditional behavior response systems (including zero tolerance), which rely heavily on aversive strategies such as detention and suspension, provide, at best, only very short-term improvements. More often, they lead to students' disengagement from school and from school-related activities, damaged relationships with teachers and administrators, the shutdown of supportive and constructive dialogue, negative self-image, and potentially worsening behaviors.

Howard Adelman and Linda Taylor, co-directors of The School Mental Health Project at UCLA, caution, "Although the intent [of such behavior response systems] is to emphasize that the *misbehavior* and its impact are bad, students too easily can experience the process as characterizing *them* as bad people" (Adelman & Taylor, 2015, p. 122). Not exactly aligned with facilitating a positive school climate, is it?

Research shows that punitive, "school pushout" forms of discipline like suspensions, expulsions, and school arrests deprive students of valuable learning time and take the greatest toll on nonwhite students, students with disabilities, LGBTQ youth, and other vulnerable student groups (Anderson, 2015). According to the Justice Policy Institute, suspending a student even once triples the likelihood that that student will end up in the juvenile justice system within a year of the suspension, and doubles the chance that that student will drop out of high school (Nelson & Lind, 2015). Nationwide, students of color are three times more likely to be suspended from school than white students, and students with disabilities are more than twice as likely to be suspended from school than students without disabilities (U.S. Department of Education, Office for Civil Rights, 2020). From this data, we can plainly see that the school-to-prison pipeline flows full of students of color, students with disabilities, and, especially, students of color who have disabilities (Nelson & Lind, 2015).

Restraint and Seclusion: What They Are and What They're *Not*

All behavior interventions must maintain a student's right to be treated safely and with dignity. Therefore, restraint and seclusion should be avoided to the greatest extent possible.

According to the U.S. Department of Education's Office for Civil Rights, "Restraint of a student means restricting the student's ability to move his or her torso, arms, legs or head freely, and seclusion of a student is confining a student alone in a room or area that he or she is not permitted to leave" (2016, p. 2). These measures are not behavioral interventions; they offer no behavioral benefit, and they put students at risk for psychological and physical harm, including trauma, severe injury, and even death. Although it may be necessary to employ restraint and seclusion techniques in extreme circumstances—that is, "situations where a student's behavior poses an imminent threat of serious physical harm to self or others" (U.S. Department of Education, 2016, p. 16)—they should never be used as disciplinary measures. They may be used only to protect the immediate safety of the individual student or others who might be in danger as a result of the student's behavior. Further, in the rare situations where a student's behavior meets that imminent threat standard, these techniques should be implemented only by school officials who have been trained to do so.

Make no mistake about this: seclusion is not the same thing as a sensory room (described in Chapter 4). A sensory room is a place that is offered to students as an optional source of comfort and sanctuary, and students in a sensory room must be free to leave it whenever they like. This is an important distinction to convey clearly to every member of the faculty and staff.

In keeping with the principles of FAPE, all programming for students on the autism spectrum should be structured such that safety interventions as extreme as restraint and seclusion are unnecessary. Any time restraint or seclusion is used, it should be viewed as indicative that that student is not receiving FAPE—that is, the educational program is not adequately meeting that student's needs. If an identified student's behaviors escalate to a level that requires restraint or seclusion, then the student is most likely in need of a more restrictive environment, and the special education evaluation team should be reconvened as soon as possible (U.S. Department of Education, 2016).

Multitiered Systems of Support (MTSS)

Most of the challenging behaviors we encounter with students on the spectrum are the result of anxiety, sensory stress, the mysteries of the hidden social and academic curricula, and an overall a lack of adequate impulse control due to executive dysfunction. These are not oppositional or defiant behaviors. And even if they were, they would still be communicative of distress. This is why zero-tolerance policies and "equal consequences for equal action" policies make no sense for these (or for most other) students.

Instead, especially in inclusive programs, we really need to remember and embody the concept that what is equal may not be fair, and what is fair may not be equal. Every one of these students has individual needs that are different from what the last student needed or what the next one will need. Thankfully, the multitiered response systems that are now in favor work beautifully not only for typical students but also for students who are on the spectrum.

Response to intervention (RTI), social-emotional learning (SEL), and school-wide positive behavior interventions and supports (SW-PBIS) all come together under the broad MTSS umbrella. What's more, all of these programs are grounded in inclusion-friendly assumptions like these:

- Different kinds of students need different kinds of interventions and supports.
- Measuring progress through clear objectives and data collection enables educators to intervene much more quickly and to greater effect.
- Students benefit from re-education more than they do from punitive responses.

Differentiation, monitoring of progress, and re-education are all critical factors in the ability of students on the spectrum to be successful in school and beyond, particularly in terms of behavior.

The Collaborative for Academic, Social, and Emotional Learning (CASEL) explains that when schoolwide SEL is implemented, its impact reverberates across academic, social, and behavioral functioning. This is because social and emotional competence is essential for all kinds of learning, as "learning is an intrinsically social and interactive process. When all students have opportunities to develop and practice social and emotional skills, mindsets, and attitudes, students are empowered, and the demands of school and life become easier to navigate" (CASEL, 2018 p. 4).

Restorative Justice

Also aligned with MTSS is the philosophy of restorative justice. Replacing the highly controversial and universally punitive zero-tolerance policies of years past, restorative justice not only addresses situations in individualized, differentiated ways but also places an emphasis on skill building and facilitating a positive, mutuality-based school culture—all indispensable factors when addressing the behaviors of students on the spectrum in an inclusive setting.

Most students on the autism spectrum won't benefit from simply being told that misbehavior is unacceptable, and they won't benefit from being punished. They need to learn why what they are doing is wrong, and they need to learn more desirable ways of handling similar situations in the future. They must be helped to develop skills they can use to regulate their own actions and reactions—everything from how to recognize when they're beginning to feel anxious, to how to communicate that feeling early and effectively and to whom. They need help accessing self-soothing and problem-solving strategies, and developing new behaviors to replace the old ones that are not serving them well. Restorative justice supports social and emotional intelligence while practicing *in situ* skill building—both critical components for the success of students who are on the spectrum. Although this system is designed to benefit everyone, its explicit, concrete, and inclusive learning emphasis is exactly the kind of intervention students on the spectrum need.

Restorative justice helps students learn what went wrong and why it was wrong, recognize who was harmed and in what way, develop new strategies for handling a situation differently in the future, and collaborate to find ways to rebuild damaged relationships. Exclusionary practices like detention, suspension, and expulsion, on the other hand, help no one learn from an experience. Whereas zero-tolerance policies deliver a short-term fix that is founded in fear, restorative justice takes a long view that is low stress, oriented toward a positive outcome, and invested in generating a growth mindset and metacognitive life skills.

Restorative justice also models a different kind of response-to-behavior framework for students who need to learn basic tenets of human interaction. Whereas zero tolerance and other punitive frameworks are vengeance based (i.e., if you cause harm, you get harmed), restorative justice is rooted in skill development, relationship, and forgiveness—all concepts that students need to practice and master. Every instance of wrongdoing is seen as an opportunity for learning, for bolstering community, and for building empathy, critical thinking, and self-control (Ashley & Burke, 2010).

Leading the Way to Successful Inclusion

As mentioned previously, many schools and districts are now implementing MTSS, which encompasses RTI, SW-PBIS, and SEL. This is a great framework for providing administrators, teachers, and students with guidelines for behavior challenges. But, just like everything else, it needs some differentiation for students on the spectrum.

Let's look now at some strategies that will help you provide differentiated support to these students and their teachers.

Crisis Versus Trauma

Acting-out behaviors can represent a crisis for students on the spectrum and for the people around them. But remember that crisis and trauma are very different things. Trauma connotes injury or pain that has long-lasting effects; crisis, on the other hand, signifies a turning point. A badly handled crisis can certainly result in trauma to the student and to others, but it doesn't have to. Instead, a crisis can and should compel a teachable moment and a learning opportunity. With historical, contextual, and individualized information at hand and differentiated strategies in place, it's entirely possible to help a student through a crisis in a way that is transcendent.

Activating Social-Emotional Learning

The most important component of MTSS for students on the spectrum is the SEL piece. Students need help learning to understand their feelings and the effects their behaviors have on others, and they need help learning to assimilate new ways of interacting and responding to challenging situations. Given those priorities, it's important to take a look at how well aligned your school's or district's disciplinary policies are with the tenets of SEL and with the needs of your inclusive student body.

Start here:

- Make sure your disciplinary standards are adequately differentiated to account for not only cultural and socioeconomic differences but developmental differences, too.
- Set the expectation that the school or district sees the restorative justice process all the way through to facilitating relationship repair.
- Build in safe, supportive, and collaborative time for faculty and staff to unpack their own actions and emotions following difficult encounters.

These three measures will give you a solid foundation for success. But there's much more you can do to calibrate your behavioral strategies and disciplinary approach to ensure a better fit—and the best support—for students on the spectrum:

- Educate a school's entire faculty and staff about the unique presentations, needs, and behaviors of students on the autism spectrum, so that their interactions with these students are productive, not destructive.
- Forewarn faculty and staff that they may need to teach and reteach new behavioral strategies a number of times before these strategies actually sink in and begin to have an effect.
- Teach students on the spectrum about *why* their behavior was unacceptable. Clarify, for example, how it impinged on the rights or comfort of others or in what ways it violated a rule.
- Always verify that these students understand lessons by having them repeat the concepts back in their own words or, if they can't use words, by demonstrating emerging behavioral skills.
- Prepare opportunities for students on the spectrum to practice executing new behavioral skills in simulated peer interactions or role-plays.

- Provide visual prompts that remind students on the spectrum what to do when actual conflicts or challenging situations that require them to apply behavioral skills arise.
- Guide students on the spectrum to cognitively file or assimilate the new behavioral concepts and skills in a way that is accessible and assimilated as a new social-emotional competency.

Let It Go

When confronted with challenging behaviors of students on the spectrum, channel your own executive function skills to stop and think. Take a moment, here, to entertain this radical possibility: Is the behavior objectively problematic—that is, dangerous, disruptive, destructive? Or might it simply be different?

Sure, teachers don't *expect* Marisol to pace across the back of the classroom during a lesson, but if she does it quietly, is that really a problem? Is the fact that Ivan needs to tap his foot while reciting the Pledge of Allegiance really disturbing anyone?

Try using this guiding principle to direct your response: *if an unusual behavior is not dangerous, disruptive, or destructive, leave it alone.* Students on the autism spectrum have enough to work on already, and you certainly have enough on your plate, too. Whenever possible, let it go. Different is OK. In fact, different is better than OK; different is what diversity and inclusivity are made of.

We can't do that! If we let Marisol pace, then everyone is going to want to be up out of their seats, too. Sound familiar? If so, encourage your teachers to explain to their students that an inclusion classroom gives every student what he or she needs. Marisol needs to pace; Naija doesn't. But when Naija needs something else, the teachers will be there to help meet her needs, too.

Remind teachers that inclusion classrooms are amalgams of many different cultures, races, religions, genders, orientations, and abilities. Right along with those differences come lots and lots of unique ways of being in the world, each one meaningful and valuable in its own way.

When It's Time to Intervene

If you determine, however, that a behavior is, in fact, *dangerous, disruptive, or destructive,* action is required. That's when it's time to intervene.

Stretch yourself to think outside the box and look for the *function* of an unusual behavior.

When students on the spectrum are breaking the rules, it is almost always for one of two reasons: either they don't fully understand the rules, or they don't have the skills necessary to be able to comply with the rules. Ross W. Greene (2014) notes that "challenging behavior occurs when the cognitive demands being placed upon a child outstrip the skills he has to respond adaptively to those demands" (p. 10). It's essential that all school staff understand that when students behave in ways that might seem like defiance or malice, what they're really showing us are signs that they need help. That's our cue to get busy reteaching the rules (and checking for understanding of the rules) and reteaching the skills (and guiding application of the skills).

One of the most crucial points to remember about intervening with behaviors of students on the spectrum is that simply *telling* them what to do differently next time will not suffice to alter their behavior. For students on the autism spectrum, even incentives cannot generate a new behavior if the requisite skills are not in place. Incentives do not teach behavior; they only increase motivation. Think of it this way: if I were offered a million dollars to write the next sentence of this book in Greek, I would be highly motivated to comply. But I would be *unable* to comply because I have never learned the Greek language.

Likewise, many of the basic skills you take for granted in your general student body may not be in place among your students on the spectrum. A behavioral goal that does not include skill building and strategies may incentivize or motivate, but *it does not teach,* and it will only increase frustration and chip away at self-esteem. Always check for skills, teach those that are needed, and provide strategies and benchmarks before setting new goals (Glanton, 2019).

Functional Behavior Assessment

Under the Individuals with Disabilities Education Act, when students with disabilities exhibit behavior that constitutes a barrier to learning for themselves or for others, the school must conduct a functional behavior assessment (FBA) and develop a behavior intervention plan (BIP).

Responding to behaviors of students who are on the spectrum requires a deep dive every single time. We really need to know the *whys* of the behavior before determining the best course of action. Really, that's true for responding to any behavior, but with students on the spectrum—because there are so many different potential triggers—it's critical that our responses are truly differentiated and individualized.

Let's take that deep dive now, so that you can be refreshed and ready to step in as problem solver, facilitator, liaison, mediator, champion, and all of the other roles you may be called upon to serve when the going gets tough.

Solving for the Function

Although students on the spectrum rarely use challenging behaviors intentionally to get attention, provoke, or get out of doing something undesirable, their behaviors nonetheless do serve a function. Most often, the function of difficult behaviors among these students is to regulate imbalances in their systems. Remember, not only do students on the spectrum struggle to manage their reactions because of executive dysfunction, but they also far prefer that their environment be calm and orderly, with strict adherence to all rules all the time. Here are some strategies for helping students on the spectrum identify their triggers and modulate their reactions, and in that way, improve their behavior.

Identify triggers. Finding out what triggered the disruptive behavior of students on the spectrum can be difficult. Their internal experience is far different from what we might expect, and their perception of an experience or interaction may be entirely different from that of others. Triggers may be things we don't notice, such as the smell of a new disinfectant in the hallway, the gentle rattling of the blinds against the window frame, or the novelty of a different brand of cups at the water cooler.

Even students who are articulate may struggle, under stress, to identify and express what it was that set them off. Be ready to support communication by using picture-communication symbols or augmentative and alternative communication devices (described in Chapter 5). Being unable to communicate can be frustrating and frightening, so be sure your faculty and staff keep alternative means of communication handy for when challenging moments arise.

Connect cause and effect. Some students who are on the spectrum may be capable of a degree of metacognition. Helping them to realize *why* they do what they do is a crucial first step in developing behavioral self-control. But keep in mind, it's a first step on a very long journey.

The sticking point is that self-reflection may be beyond most students on the spectrum. The cognitive-behavioral connections may elude them, and they may be unable to apply abstract analysis to their impulse-driven, sensory-oriented, anxiety-fueled systems.

However, the majority of students on the spectrum can and should learn to make concrete connections between cause and effect, and they can learn to substitute certain behaviors for others in an environment that supports their needs.

In a calm and quiet moment, you or trusted teachers or counselors can help students examine the disconnect between an accumulation of small upsets and a big reaction, or between a trigger and an out-of-control reaction. A cause and-effect schema, supplemented as needed by picture-based communication symbols, would be useful here. Here are some guidelines:

- Point out how the cause and effect were mismatched, and work with the student to identify an effect (a reaction) that might have been a better fit for the cause (the trigger).
- Ask for the student's input about what happened. As mentioned previously, be sure you have PC symbols or other augmentative and alternative communication devices handy to facilitate this important step.
- Give the student plenty of time to digest your suggestions and respond at their own pace and in their own way.
- Ask for feedback. What do they think about the situation? How do they *feel* about the situation? Do they agree with the analysis provided? Again, be sure to provide opportunities for facilitated communication as needed.
- If possible, involve the student in planning and effecting changes that might improve the situation in the future. Some students may benefit from tools that help them to monitor their own mood escalation and provide guidance as to when and how they can signal to others that they need help. You can find an assortment of regulation-related reproducibles and other creative tools for students and teachers in the Resources section at http://barbaraboroson.com.
- Be aware that debriefing strategies will definitely not be effective for students on the spectrum *during* behavioral outbursts, and they may not be effective for some even after calm has been restored. Be patient, supporting coping strategies, until equilibrium is restored, before trying to elicit productive reflection.

Pursue patterns. One simple but effective way of approaching functional behavior assessment with students on the spectrum is to lead your teachers and staff in considering the antecedents of the student's reactive behavior in the context of the 5 Ws: *who, what, when, where,* and *why.*

The 5 Ws

Just as investigative reporters and journalists must hit all of the 5 Ws in order to deliver meaningful context to a hot news story, inclusive educators need to investigate all of these areas in order to develop a complete understanding of what might have triggered a certain behavior. Gather an interdisciplinary team to look closely for patterns and to brainstorm workarounds and solutions. Be sure to consult closely with parents or guardians—not only to keep them in the loop, but also because they are indispensable sources of information regarding known triggers for their children. Figure 7.1 (see pp. 132–133) provides an overview of the 5 Ws in functional behavior assessment, listing specific questions and considerations. Here is additional information to keep in mind, along with some practical guidance.

Who. The *who* questions are designed to determine whether certain people are commonly present before or during behavioral outbursts—but not to assign blame. Please make it crystal clear to teachers and other staff that this process is in no way a blame game. (In fact, a nice touch is to offer a small prize to the teacher or staff member who learns or grows the most from a debriefing session!)

Remind your teachers to be honest with themselves and each other while asking *who* questions. Students may react differently to certain faculty members, staff members, peers, or administrators. A behavior could be a response to a pattern of teasing by a certain peer. It could be a sensory reaction to the squeaking Styrofoam coffee cup one teacher always carries around or to the aroma of an aide's hand lotion. It could be that another teacher stands a bit too close for comfort. In cases where a teacher or staff member does turn out to be the common denominator in a student's negative behaviors, small adaptive changes could be in everyone's best interest. For example, simply investing in a reusable, squeakless coffee cup would benefit not only that student but the environment, too.

What. The *what* questions guide us to look at the context around the acting-out behavior. What is happening before, during, and as a result of the behavior?

Figure 7.1: The 5Ws as a Guide to Functional Behavior Assessment

	Key Questions	**Considerations**
Who	• Who tends to be in proximity to the student when the problematic behavior occurs? • Who tends to be nearby shortly before the problematic behavior occurs? • Are there specific teachers or aides who tend to be involved when problematic behaviors occur?	• Certain students may be bullying the student on the spectrum. Remember, bullying may be invisible. Look *and* listen closely. • Certain students may be provoking the student on the spectrum. Small, quiet affronts can really add up. • Certain adults may present inconsistent expectations, speak too loudly, or stand too close for comfort. Be sure everyone who works with this student is educated as to how best to support students on the autism spectrum.
What	• What are the circumstances surrounding the student at the time of the problematic behavior? • What warning signs tend to occur before the problematic behavior? • What happens as a result of a student's problematic behavior?	• Certain situations may be triggering because they are too loud, too quiet, too crowded, too chaotic, too smelly, etc. • Some students may speak loudly, pace, shut down, or exhibit more self-stimulatory behaviors as tension escalates. • If responses to the problematic behavior are not addressing the root causes or functions of the behavior, it will continue or escalate further.
When	• Does the problematic behavior tend to happen more during transitional *times?* • Does it tend to happen more often on transitional *days?* • Does it tend to happen before or after specific activities	• Common pinch points are the bus ride, arrival, lunch time (before, during, and after), and dismissal. • Days that are adjacent to weekends or vacations may be challenging as students transition from changes in structure and routine between school and home. • Anticipatory anxiety or reactive of stress may trigger problematic behaviors.

Key Questions	Considerations
Where • Does the problematic behavior tend to occur in the classroom or in another specific environment? • Does the problematic behavior tend to happen in unstructured places, like the cafeteria, playground, hallway, or bus? • Does the problematic behavior tend to occur in certain special area classes?	• Therapeutic services, modifications, and accommodations are mandated because they are necessary. Be sure those supports are being provided as required. • Is the student in need of more supervision, support, or structure during less structured activities? • There may be specific sensory or social challenges in certain special area classes like art or PE. Also, special area teachers may not be implementing the same structures and supports that are benefiting the student in the classroom.

Key Questions	Considerations
Why • Why is this problematic behavior happening? • What is the student trying to communicate through this behavior? What is the function of the behavior? • What small or large changes must be made to eliminate the *need* for this behavior?	• Add up *all* of the patterns noted in this investigative process. • What specific distress is this difficult behavior communicating to us? What *function* is behavior serving? • Review findings during team meetings, revising and reiterating supports and structures and ensuring their consistent application across contexts. Formulate a BIP based on findings and track progress in terms of frequency, duration, and intensity. If the behavior persists despite the FBA and the BIP, consider the possibility that the environment may not be restrictive enough.

Sometimes we worry that removing an acting-out student from a stressful situation will inadvertently reinforce the acting-out behavior. For example, maybe we respond to Matty's tantrum by providing some stimulus-free quiet time but in doing so, we fear that we are rewarding his tantrum. Rather than think of the quiet time as an undeserved reward, think of it as a valuable solution. The tantrum was giving us information: *This situation is overwhelming. I need a break.* Use that information to become proactive. Build in those much-needed breaks preemptively so that Matty doesn't resort to acting out in order to get the relief he needs.

Or adapt the situation so that it isn't so overwhelming to Matty.

Or create a system through which Matty can request and reliably be granted certain kinds of breaks without having to resort to escalated behaviors.

Nothing Personal

Because the responses of students on the spectrum are not in their control—unless they have developed adequate skills for executive function, coping, and behavior regulation—their acting-out behaviors should not be taken personally by those who work with them. Carole Schaffan, a principal at a school in South Dakota, told me about her experience:

> I used to take everything as a personal slight to me. Whenever students would make rude comments, ignore me, or refuse to do what I asked, I was shocked that they would act that way with me when we had a close relationship. I have since learned that they are not acting out to get back at me; they are just acting the only way they know how.

When. When thinking about w*hen,* consider not only clock time but also types of time, such as transitional time, pressured time, unstructured time, and so on. If the difficult behavior tends to be worse on Mondays, for example, it's possible that the student is reacting to an absence of clear structure at home over the weekend. In that case, consider helping the family learn about using a visual schedule at home. Another reason behaviors at school may be worse on Mondays could be that returning to school is the stressor. Ask the school social worker or counselor to look into issues at school and home that could contribute to this kind of transitional stress.

Where. As you consider the *where* questions, be mindful of the fact that locations that might not seem overwhelming to you could be utterly overwhelming to your students on the spectrum. Lots of behavior triggers lurk in the lunchroom and the playground or other outdoor areas. Those locations, often less supervised and more chaotic, impose innumerable social and sensory demands on these students. Observe what's happening in the lunchroom and outside. Ask the aides and teachers what they are seeing. It's almost always advisable to assign additional helpers to lunch and recess who know not only whom to help but *how* to help them. Consider soliciting student volunteers for this job, too. (See Chapter 5 for more ideas along these lines.)

Balancing the Tray

A behavior and its triggers may have no apparent connection. When a student throws a shoe across the room, it's easy to assume that there was a knot in the lace, that the tongue was stuck, or that there was some other shoe-related snafu. But more often, disruptive behaviors are the result of the mounting pressure from numerous small affronts to a student's equilibrium.

Lenore Gerould (1996) compares the accumulation of small stressors to balancing a tray of water glasses on one hand. Each student seeks to keep their own tray balanced, but every upsetting event is like another glass of water added to the tray. Some glasses are heavier and fuller than others, and the student must constantly try to adapt and cope as the tray gets increasingly wobbly. In the end, it takes only one more glass to topple the tray and send everything crashing down. That last glass may not have been the heaviest or the fullest; it was just the one that was added right before the fall.

Why. Ultimately, the goal is to determine *why the student is exhibiting the disruptive behavior.* Adding up the conclusions of the *who, what, when,* and *where* analysis should yield plenty of contextual data to help you determine the *why.*

Once we identify the offending triggers, the temptation is to simply make adjustments so that trigger doesn't interfere with the student's functioning. A staff member can easily switch to an unscented hand lotion if that's the issue. And that's a great start. But that doesn't help the student to learn better ways of coping with the smell of hand lotions yet to come. For that, we need to teach some new skills. For that, we need a behavior intervention plan.

Regular Kid Stuff

Given that there are so many idiosyncrasies and unusual behaviors in the mix with students on the spectrum, professionals often look for zebras instead of horses when they hear the sound of hoofbeats. Remember that even though these students may have complex diagnoses, they can have very basic "regular kid" problems, too. As Polimeni, Richdale, and Francis (2005) point out, behavioral reactions may be due to "normal" triggers, including hunger, thirst, allergies, headache, earache, sore throat, fatigue, or stomachache. Students on the spectrum are three times more likely to have stomach problems than their neurotypical peers and one-and-one-half times more likely to have sleep problems.

Behavior Intervention Plans

A BIP emerges from the interdisciplinary team's FBA in conjunction with evidence-based data that has been collected and in collaboration with parents or guardians. The plan must be completely customized to address the very specific triggers and reactive patterns of the individual student.

The BIP should address common antecedents, the resultant behaviors, and the natural consequences that may inadvertently reinforce the challenging behaviors. It must include an objective system for measuring progress, as well as a schedule for reviewing and adjusting the plan as needed. The goal of the BIP is not only to prevent challenging behaviors by meeting the student's underlying needs but also to teach more adaptive replacement behaviors.

Make sure your BIP contains the following components:

- *Differentiated behavioral antecedent interventions,* such as "The student will have access to icons to bolster his ability to communicate distress."
- *Differentiated self-regulatory strategies,* such as "The student will stop and count to 10 before beginning any new assignment or task."
- *Differentiated replacement behaviors,* such as "The student will raise two fingers to communicate that they need time in the sensory room."
- *Differentiated reinforcement strategies,* such as "The teacher will provide verbal praise, using a ratio of at least four positive comments to one correction."

Behavior plans are most effective when they are implemented across contexts. Students should encounter identical or equivalent sets of expectations in every environment throughout the inclusive school building, as well as on the bus and at home.

After serious incidents, it's essential to debrief with faculty and staff. Always touch base to ensure that they are physically and emotionally well. In some cases, they may be feeling overwhelmed, shaken up, frightened, or hopeless. Support those who need help, thank those who stepped in to help, create a plan of action that will serve everyone better in the future, and determine as a group how you will all work together even better next time.

Spectrum Safety

One frequent and frightening behavior that is common to students on the autism spectrum is wandering (also known as "eloping"). In the same way that these students tend to get preoccupied in pursuing their own cognitive or conversational directions, they may pursue their own physical directions as well. According to the Autism Wander Awareness Alerts Response and Education (AWAARE) Collaboration (n.d.):

continued

Spectrum Safety (*continued*)

- Nearly half of children with autism engage in wandering behavior.
- Wandering occurs across all settings, under every type of adult supervision.
- Increased risks are associated with autism severity.
- Half of families report they have never received advice or guidance about wandering from a professional.
- Accidental drowning accounts for approximately 90 percent of lethal outcomes.

In response to these alarming statistics, the National Autism Association (NAA) has created the BeRedy Booklet for Teachers, which is full of useful school-related tips and strategies and available as a free download from the NAA website.

Students on the spectrum tend to be drawn to bodies of water. Especially if your school or schools are anywhere near an ocean, lake, bay, river, pond, or even a creek—and even if you're not—*please* put these measures in place. No school leader would allow a school building to function without operational smoke alarms. In an inclusive program, these safety precautions are equally critical and require the same level of attention.

Consequential Clarity

As discussed earlier in this book, students on the spectrum are not likely to recognize the emotions that are embedded in your tone, in the volume of voice, in your posture, or in the expression on your face. That's all part of the hidden curriculum. Your quiet praise—and, by equal measure, your quiet displeasure—may not be enough.

Keep it concrete. Pair praise or disapproval with meaningful, concrete reinforcers that will give students the unequivocal message of your approval or disapproval. Of course, the goal with all students is that they learn to self-regulate because it's simply the "right" thing to do. Ultimately, we want to create conscientious adults who have integrity and who will be good and kind citizens, even when no one is watching. But because some students on the spectrum may not understand abstract values like "the greater good" or the concepts of altruism and integrity, for now they will need concrete incentives to improve challenging behaviors.

Keep it straightforward. Avoid using sarcasm with students on the spectrum. In fact, avoid using sarcasm with all students. You just never know how your words will be understood or misunderstood, how your intention might be represented or misrepresented, or when you might inadvertently touch a nerve.

Keep it logical. Given the combined challenges of concrete thinking and mind-blindness (see Chapter 5), students on the spectrum will learn best from very specific, natural consequences because they follow logically from the infraction. A student on the spectrum would generally not infer any meaningful connection between, say, shoving another student during softball at recess and having to stay after school for detention four hours later.

Keep it connected. Try to keep the consequence properly scaled to the infraction. In this example, taking away the student's right to play softball for a day or two—while they are taught a new protocol about interacting respectfully with others during softball—would be a meaningful response; taking away *recess* would not.

Recess: Non-Negotiable

Never, ever remove recess as a consequence for bad behavior! Students on the spectrum, and other students who may misbehave, absolutely must have an outlet for their excess energy. Withholding that outlet not only is certain to backfire, but also removes opportunities for learning. Instead, just take away free *access* to certain problematic activities at recess (like softball, as per the example above), and only during the period of active skill and behavior remediation. Add supervision and facilitation by adults or designated responsible students. Unless you want your students to try to hold their ya-yas in, let them let them out!

Measuring Progress

Once new behavioral plans and strategies are in place, watching for progress can be discouraging, because progress for students on the spectrum can be excruciatingly slow. Sometimes we give up far too soon. For example, when dealing with a situation in which a student is flipping desks, we are likely to create an emergency intervention plan and then look for an immediate cessation of that behavior. If there are repeat episodes of desk flipping, we often abandon our plan.

However, as urgent as it is that the specific behavior cease, there may be improvements in certain *aspects* of the behavior that are being overlooked. For example, perhaps prior to the intervention this student was flipping desks twice a week. Now, maybe it's still happening, but only once a week. Still problematic, to be sure, but a significant improvement. Or maybe the behavior is still happening twice a week, but now it takes staff only three minutes to defuse the situation, whereas it used to take seven. That's progress right there.

Be sure to build these three progress checkpoints into the BIP, and call them out when you see them:

- *Frequency.* How often does the behavior occur? Track how many times a particular behavior occurs in a day, in a week, in a month.
- *Duration.* How long does the behavior last? Note how long the behavior persists each time it emerges.
- *Intensity.* How bad does the situation get? Consider the severity of the behavior on a scale of 1 to 10, with 1 indicating a mildly disruptive behavior and 10 meaning a frightening, destructive, or dangerous behavior.

Consider improvements in any of these areas to be movement in the right direction. Remember that in the business of growing humans, progress happens one step at a time.

● ▲ ◆ ◀ ■

This chapter offered a number of ways to help preempt and respond to disruptive behaviors. However, one of your best resources for ameliorating these behaviors is coming up in the next chapter, which is all about parents and guardians. There, we'll explore some of the common issues that confront parents and guardians and the common conundrums those issues pose in the interactions between educators and parents. Learn how to harness the wisdom of parents and guardians to get ahead of disruptive behaviors and shift the home-school collaboration from confounding to constructive.

Parents and Guardians

Among the profound spectrum-related challenges described in this book, there is one particular challenge that inclusive teachers and administrators all over the world describe as the most vexing and intractable in their work with students who are on the autism spectrum. It's not academics or differentiation. It's not struggles with sensation or communication or socialization. It's not even behavior.

It's people like me. It's their parents and guardians.

Teachers ask this earnest question: "What do we do when parents just can't hear our concerns about their kids?"

To answer this question, we need to understand the complex places these parents are coming from. We need to understand what they need from us, we need to consider their needs in the context of their child within the inclusive school community, and we need to find ways to work productively together as true partners. This is especially important when working with students on the spectrum, who depend on continuity of expectations across environments. Schools and families really must be on the same page. Indeed, many of the issues addressed in this chapter are specific to families of students who are on the autism spectrum or have other special needs. But taking a little time to consider the unique contexts and perspectives of *every* family will optimize the success of all of your students and enrich your entire inclusive school community.

Decoding the Perspectives of Parents and Guardians of Students on the Spectrum

As different as the parents and guardians of our students may be, for the most part they really want the same thing: what's best for their own kids. Complicating the picture, however, is that many of their kids need different things: some need a bit of nurturing, a little encouragement, or a vote of confidence; others need a new school or class placement, alternative teaching styles, assistive technology, behavioral intervention, or special accommodations; and others need a stable role model, a safe place, or a roof over their heads. More complicated still, many parents and guardians have very different ideas than the school does about what their kids need and about what school can and should provide.

Although it is not incumbent on schools to meet every one of these needs, we should be all-in on supporting the well-being of the whole child—not only because we want our students to be ready to learn, but also because, as educators, we care.

The Things They Carry

Although parents and guardians may share long-term goals of happiness and success for their children, their ideas about how to get there and their attitudes toward school, education, and disability are as variable as the students we serve. When we encounter parents who seem resistant, oppositional, hostile, or unresponsive to our outreach, we must consider the demands that having a child with autism or other significant special needs place on families.

Depending on where parents and guardians are in their personal journey, some may get teary every time you introduce a new issue of concern because they just cannot handle one more thing. Others may flatly deny or reject your interpretations because the child you describe doesn't resemble the one they know at home. Others can't bear to hear anything negative because they are too deeply invested in the notion of their child as an idealized reflection of themselves. Still others have learned to be afraid of labels or medication and refuse to have their child evaluated for fear of what might come of it. Let's look a little more closely at some of the special challenges these parents and guardians may be dealing with and at ways you can support and join forces with them, wherever they are.

Feelings of Grief and Loss

Consider the moment in which these parents were told or came to the realization that their perfect little child, born with 10 fingers, 10 toes, and infinite possibility, actually has a pervasive neurodevelopmental disorder. For many parents of children with significant special needs, the diagnosis of a lifelong disability is akin to a death.

It represents the sudden shattering of hopes, dreams, and legacy. Often parents go through a lengthy and agonizing grief process that includes intense periods of denial, anger, self-blame, depression, and more before they can begin to accept what is, as well as what may never be.

Consider, too, the guardian—a grandparent or other relative, a family friend or foster parent—who has willingly or reluctantly taken on the responsibility of a child who comes to them with needs that far exceed those of typical children. Moreover, going into guardianship can be especially disorienting and upsetting to children on the autism spectrum, who struggle to cope with change. They have most likely lost their prior parent or caregiver, changed homes, and been separated from siblings, pets, and comfort objects.

Parents and guardians of these children have to kick into high gear. Just living with and raising a child on the spectrum 24/7 can be a physically and emotionally debilitating experience. In addition, they must learn about and wend their way through serpentine bureaucratic systems to round up suitable services, shouting their child's challenges out to the universe in search of help. Extended family, if there are any, may bring to bear the pressure of cultural, generational, or other biases, wrongfully shaming the family for poor parenting or discouraging them from pursuing help from a distrusted medical establishment.

Obtaining services is time-consuming and costly—and rarely well supported by medical insurance—so a heavy financial burden likely weighs on the family as well. All of this is in addition to the everyday needs of a typical family, including those of the child's siblings, who often get lost in the shuffle. And along the way, these families may have encountered assorted professionals who are far less accepting, flexible, knowledgeable, kind, and collaborative than you are. Given these overwhelming, unrelenting, and complicated circumstances, it's perfectly reasonable that many of these parents and guardians present as highly anxious, depressed, or wary. They have good reason to be afraid, sad, stoic, angry, or skeptical.

Feelings of Marginalization and Difference

Just like their special kids, these parents and guardians may be marginalized or feel like hangers-on in the school community. They have watched other people's children having playdates, getting invited to birthday parties, and excelling in sports, and they hurt for their children. Further, because many parent relationships form through the children, they themselves feel the hurt of being left out of opportunities for social camaraderie.

Parents are *constantly* judged by the characters and behaviors of their children. So when a child who perseverates on smells goes around sniffing people and telling them what they smell like, that child's parents know that the behavior reflects right back on them. Many parents and guardians of students on the spectrum worry about their child standing out or acting up during school events. A school concert is all stress for these parents as they spend the evening gripping the arms of their chairs, braced for the possibility that their child will start doing the Renegade dance in the middle of "The Hallelujah Chorus."

Feelings of Intimidation and Unworthiness

Some parents and guardians feel intimidated by the school and by school personnel, and unworthy of providing feedback or making suggestions. Especially when speaking to education leaders, many parents and guardians may believe that, given your expertise and credentials, they cannot possibly have anything of value to offer. These parents may assume that if you're having trouble with their kid at school, that's not something they can have any influence on.

Even more than parents of typical kids, parents of children on the spectrum are especially likely to feel ineffective and incapable because their children are not doing what other kids are able to do and not developing in expectable ways. Even though autism is definitely not caused by any particular parenting style, these parents may feel that they have failed to parent their children effectively.

Be aware that, even though these parents and guardians may feel intimidated or unworthy, they may, paradoxically, present as aggressive. Feeling ineffective is a terrible feeling; it's infuriating. When you meet aggression from parents, consider—even though this may feel counterintuitive to you—that the aggression may be coming from a place of self-doubt and despair.

Feelings of Doubt and Suspicion

Other parents or guardians may feel threatened by your status as part of "the system," the establishment. Due to that association, they may view you and all other educators with doubt and suspicion. Many families have good reason to be distrustful of systems. Consider that "systems" check up on whether families have a legitimate address in their district. "Systems" come into their homes and check on their parent-ing skills. "Systems" deny people unemployment benefits and healthcare. "Systems" threaten families with deportation.

With this in mind, it's understandable that parents and guardians—even those who do not have children on the autism spectrum—sometimes band together around conspiracy theories, such as these:

- Schools don't want what's best for the students.
- Schools are trying to turn kids into robots.
- Teachers only care about getting tenure.
- Teachers are trying to turn kids against their families.

These mindsets can be reinforced when parents and guardians see that educators are teaching ideas that may be unfamiliar to them or that are not in step with their own culture, ideologies, family practices, or family values.

Many ASD-specific interventions—such as assistive technology or occupational therapy strategies like wearing a weighted vest or brushing for desensitization—may seem strange or dubious. Parents and guardians who tend to be distrustful of the school may greet those kinds of hard-won accommodations with great skepticism or even refusal.

Not only do these negative perceptions interfere with open collaboration between home and school, but you can bet they infiltrate the relationship between students and teachers. Kids in these situations often end up feeling disloyal to their parents by liking their teachers or by enjoying school.

Feelings of Disdain and Resentment

In any family—with or without children on the autism spectrum—parents and guardians may have had negative experiences with school as students themselves, which can make them predisposed to be resentful. Maybe they dropped out because they felt no one at school cared. Maybe they were bullied or discriminated against at school and adopted a me-against-the-world perspective. Or perhaps they failed at school and decided that school doesn't matter—or that only practical skills are worth learning.

Unconvinced of the inherent value of education, these parents and guardians may take a very hands-off attitude toward school. As a result, they're not inclined to form partnerships with educators. They may view school and home as entirely separate entities that have little or nothing to do with each other: *I'm getting him up in the morning, getting him to school on time. The rest is your job. Not my problem.*

When a family like this has a child on the spectrum, this scenario can be reinforced by the fact that these parents are not seeing the progress and growth in their child that is evident in neurotypical children. Their child is not a poster child for the effectiveness of education, and that only underlines their skepticism.

Feelings of Exhaustion and Hopelessness

Like all families, the families of students on the spectrum may be dealing with any number of hardships that we know little about. Many families struggle with relationship difficulties, the challenges of single parenthood, unemployment or the stress of juggling multiple jobs, or economic disadvantage. Some grapple with discrimination, physical or mental illness, violence, substance abuse, or immigration status. Then, on top of everything else, there are the relentless challenges of rearing a child who is on the spectrum. Janet Ferone, a founding administrator of alternative and inclusion programs for Boston Public Schools, provided me this snapshot of what life is like for families they serve, who face hardship upon hardship:

> In addition to autism, our families face many obstacles to getting needed services, and students return home from school to often chaotic, high-stress homes. Most students are not with two biological parents but are often raised by grandmothers or single moms who are struggling to make ends meet and often live in high crime areas where safe community access is limited. So, after a full school day of highly structured, positive interactions with an eye toward socialization and transitions to the community, students often spend hours at home isolated in front of the TV, repetitively watching videos and cartoons or doing other screen-based, noninteractive activities.

Many of our students from immigrant families must deal with cultural attitudes about autism, with family members not understanding the diagnosis and feeling like more discipline is the answer. They may face discrimination based on disability as well as racial and ethnic identity. Additionally, families who don't speak English have difficulty attaining a complete understanding of what they hear from the school and even greater difficulty expressing their concerns and questions to you in the precise way they might in their native language.

Life at home with a child on the autism spectrum can be exhausting and overwhelming. The hours when that child is at school may be the only respite these parents get from rigidity, perseveration, and tantrums. Communications from school often pile on to that high level of baseline stress. Parents and guardians of students on the spectrum may hear no good news at all from school related to their kids. When all the calls from school are reporting bad news and heaping more worries on their shoulders, these parents and guardians can begin to pull away.

Feelings of Urgency and Frustration

While most children move from grade to grade in a straightforward, linear fashion, students on the spectrum require very specific program considerations and adjustments every year and even throughout the year. In many cases, especially in poorly funded or overwhelmed districts, the appropriateness of a child's services is commensurate with the effectiveness of the advocacy of their parents or guardians.

The burden of obtaining optimal services weighs heavily on many parents and guardians—including those who know exactly what's available and what to ask for, and those who know that there is much they don't know. Most parents and guardians worry that there is more they should be doing for their children and that there is more the school could be doing for their children. Unlike parents of typical kids, these parents feel the clock ticking on the time they have left to intervene to change the course of their child's development in critical ways. They get rightfully impatient and frustrated when services are not provided as mandated, when evaluations and meetings are delayed, when beloved and effective service providers are reassigned, when they feel their input is being ignored by the school, or when their child is denied access to services and opportunities that stand a chance of making a difference.

Be mindful of where the parents and guardians have been, and meet them where they are as you work together to support their children.

Life at School, Life at Home, and Everything in Between

Now that we know a bit more about where these parents are coming from, let's look at what might be going awry in home school collaboration.

Educators and parents or guardians often experience the same student in vastly different ways. Sometimes it seems we are not even talking about the same kid at all.

Doubt and distrust, often triggered by underlying feelings of inadequacy, as discussed previously, can flare up unexpectedly on *both* sides of this dyad. Educators as well as parents and guardians are vulnerable to feeling criticized and disrespected. When defensiveness rears its head, it can contaminate the relationship between educators and parents and slam shut any hope of meaningful collaboration going forward.

The first step in breaking through this negative spiral is to acknowledge that students can, indeed, function in vastly differing ways in the separate contexts of home and school. As educators, we need to accept that parents and guardians really may be seeing a very different child than we see at school. And they, too, need to understand that educators may be seeing a very different child at school than they see at home. The nature of the differences can vary, depending on an individual child's strengths and challenges and even depending on the day. Reports of extreme differences in functioning can be difficult for us to believe or accept; however, they may be very real and very valid.

Let's unpack these differing experiences and start to put those doubts to rest.

"It's All Cool at School"

Some students on the spectrum function pretty well in school. In these situations, the teacher experiences the student as attentive, cooperative, flexible, and engaged—they may even wonder why such a student has been given an ASD diagnosis. As educators, it's easy to be lulled into believing that we know the whole child. It's tempting to assume that this student functions at this same, relatively high level across contexts. But, in fact, some students may function entirely differently at home, and their parents may find them to be exasperating and exhausting for a number of reasons.

Structure. At school, life follows a reliable and comprehensible schedule. *First, we hang up our backpacks; then it's circle time.* Or, *First period is science; then comes art; and then it's English.* Or, *If it's Friday, it must be Pizza Day. It says so on the calendar.* Better yet, the school schedule may be presented in a visual, digital, or other multisensory format that promotes engagement and bolsters comprehension. This kind of transparent structure is very grounding for students on the spectrum and may make a critical functional difference.

At home, on the other hand, parents may have a more laid-back culture. Chances are the dinner menu isn't posted a month in advance. As comfortable as an easygoing home may be for most of us, it may not be the best thing for everyone. In a sense, students on the spectrum can actually be more relaxed when the environment around them is *less* relaxed: the more clearly structured their environment, the more readily they can relax within that structure.

Best foot forward. Another reason some children function better at school than at home is that often they give school all they've got, and then absolutely fall apart at home. It's not easy for parents when their kids come home like little tornadoes. Empathize with these parents who are wrung out, but also reassure them that their children have their priorities in order. These kids are bringing their best selves to school. That's what we all do. We put our best self out into the world, and then we let it all hang out at home. Home should be a safe and forgiving place to let loose and blow off steam at the end of a hard day's work.

The parents or guardians in situations like these may doubt or challenge your upbeat characterizations. For example, on hearing your glowing report, they may feel skeptical: *There is no way that my child patiently waits her turn for the computer at school when at home she shoves her sister out of the chair.* They may feel suspicious: *This teacher must have very low expectations for my child because she's been labeled autistic; this school has given up on her.* They may feel self-doubt: *If this teacher can get my child to cooperate, why can't I? What am I doing wrong? Am I too passive? Too strict? Am I a bad parent? Is this all my fault?*

As a leader, listen carefully, in situations like these, for feelings of skepticism, suspicion, and self-doubt, and tell your teachers to do the same.

It's important to be careful in dynamics like these. Educators tend to make assumptions about parents and guardians when a seemingly docile student is causing difficulty at home. And although few would ever speak this judgment aloud, it often comes across loud and clear. Any time a parent responds defensively to positive reports or resists suggestions of things to try at home, we educators need to check ourselves and be honest. Are we—deep down—feeling judgy? If so, disdain and disrespect are probably seeping through our carefully cultivated professional veneer.

Let's set judgment aside and instead looks for ways to share resources and strategies so that our students can generalize their school success to their home environment.

"It's All Good in the Hood"'

Even more common is the opposite scenario: a student is struggling significantly at school, but parents or guardians maintain that everything is just fine at home, *thank you very much.* At school, this is a child who is constantly up disturbing others, cannot sit still or work independently even for a minute. *What?! Not* my *kid! My kid can read a whole book independently at home!*

As educators, we need to check ourselves here, too. We might be inclined to doubt the parents' account since it's so different from what we see. In fact—let's be really honest—we might even think: *Denial.* Well, sometimes there *is* a component of denial. Remember, no parents want to hear that their child is struggling or falling short. If you believe denial is part of the picture, don't roll your eyes and sigh. Instead, work with it. Gently help these parents to come to terms with their child's challenges, using the strategies you'll find later in this chapter.

But more often, in this situation, a child *really is* more focused and engaged at home than at school. In some cases, home may be profoundly individualized, and this can make all the difference. At home, family members can (and need to) do whatever works, just to get through the day. My friend Sasha puts her daughter's book on the floor and lets her read in a handstand position because that's the only way her daughter will do her reading homework. That degree of flexibility may be the reason a child really *can* read a whole book independently at home.

One family I worked with had fallen into a routine in which Rahul, their child on the spectrum, was always allowed to choose the family game—and would always get to go first. His parents and siblings had learned the hard way that it was easier to let Rahul have his way; trying to be fair and letting someone else go first was simply not worth the battle. If Rahul didn't get to go first, the entire day could be ruined for the whole family. Many families have learned what works to keep their children calm—and they are often very eager to share that vital information with you so that their children can get through the school day without, say, biting anyone.

Lost in Transition

In addition to the challenges that can arise from the differences between school and home, sometimes unclear or inaccurate information—as conveyed by students from one venue to the other—is at the heart of misunderstandings between school and home. Despite their best intentions, students on the autism spectrum can be particularly unreliable conduits of information from school to home and home to school, due to difficulties with receptive and expressive language, auditory processing, engagement, and organization. Often the information parents or guardians get from their kids or that teachers get from their students is just patently wrong or totally skewed. Teachers need to keep in close touch with these parents in order to ensure that accurate information is being shared between home and school. Figure 8.1 lists some common obstacles to home-school communication, their effects, and some ways to work around them.

These challenges mean that these parents tend to get less accurate information than most, even though they have much more to worry about than most. Kids on the spectrum get confused and disoriented. They lose their stuff, they lose their way, and they lose control. They misunderstand and miscommunicate. They get bullied and teased and overstimulated and overwhelmed on a regular basis. This makes life very, very challenging for them at school. The least restrictive environment mandate of the Individuals with Disabilities Education Act ensures that these students are being stretched to capacity and sometimes beyond. And that means that, in an inclusive program, there is no such thing as a "typical" day for these atypical children.

Once, in 8th grade, my son came home from school extremely agitated, insisting that everyone in our family needed to pack a bag immediately. He said his social studies teacher had told the class that a bus would be picking us up at our house in an hour because we were all being relocated. He insisted that this was the case, even as I kept explaining that it made no sense. I tried to reason with him: *We didn't sign any kind of permission slip. . . . Buses don't stop at our house. . . . Your teacher can't tell your parents what to do.* But he was utterly insistent and growing increasingly anxious.

As he began frantically packing, I called the school; thankfully, I was able to reach his teacher. She told me that they had been discussing the mandatory evacuations that occurred in Europe during World War II, and that she had presented a "what if" scenario to the class: *What if your family were told that they had an hour to evacuate?*

Figure 8.1: Information-Sharing Challenges to Home-School Collaboration

Area of Challenge	How the Challenge Manifests	Effect on Home-School Collaboration	Ways to Support Home-School Collaboration
Speech and language	Students on the autism spectrum may be non-verbal or struggle with communication challenges related to receptive language, auditory processing, or pragmatic language.	These students may be unable to convey to their parents what was said in class, or unable to convey it accurately. By the same token, they may be unable to tell you or their teachers accurately what was said at home.	Reinforce important information in a communication log that students can refer to if they don't process or file the words properly in their minds. If you receive questionable information, assume error, not malice!
Organization	Students on the autism spectrum may be highly disorganized. Important information can be shoved into random places, never to be seen again.	Important information may not survive the multi-step journey into the backpack, out of the backpack, into parents' or guardians' hands, and then back to school, so communication can get derailed in either direction.	Designate and label a consistent, reliable place in a student's backpack for keeping important information so that it will be readily retrievable. Back up important messages via e-mail or an online portal, *even through high school,* to keep parents in the loop.
Engagement	Students on the autism spectrum may be intensely preoccupied with their own repetitive thoughts and ideas and therefore inadequately engaged or attentive to important information being presented to them.	Essential details may not be effectively received or retained. For example, the teacher alerts students to bring a bag lunch on the museum trip and that there will be no access to refrigerators. The student on the spectrum hears "museum," thinks, *Ooh, dinosaurs!* and misses the entire message about lunch.	Highlight information that needs to be attended to either verbally or visually. Make sure students have absorbed the necessary information by having them restate or write it down in their own words.

Area of Challenge	How the Challenge Manifests	Effect on Home-School Collaboration	Ways to Support Home-School Collaboration
Executive function	Students on the autism spectrum struggle with distinguishing important from less important information and with skills like reading between the lines, generalizing information, and seeing the big picture. Because they tend to be concrete thinkers, unspoken messages may go unnoted.	Even if a student is engaged enough to receive and retain the teacher's reminder to bring a bag lunch on the museum trip, the implied message about no refrigerators (i.e., "don't bring anything perishable") may not be intuited.	Present important messages in clear, simple, specific, and comprehensive terms, saying what you mean. Encourage questions for clarification and check for understanding.

How would you feel? What would you pack? As is often the case, my son had retained these details but missed the big picture.

This sort of communication problem goes both ways. Sometimes the information you get from students is wrong. When a student tells you that his parent said something that shocks or insults you, please assume that it's an inadvertent distortion by the student rather than malice from the parent. If a student comes to school saying, "My mom said you remind her of a dog," try not to take immediate offense. Instead, dig a little deeper. Remember, because of mindblindness, this child does not understand how his comment will be perceived by you and so doesn't realize how it might have been better proffered. One or two more questions from you might reveal that your last name is the same as the name, of the mother's childhood dog, and so every time she hears your name, she reflects fondly on her youth.

Leading the Way to Successful Inclusion

Forging productive relationships with parents and guardians is not only best practice, but also necessary for providing wraparound support for students on the spectrum. Let's look at strategies for building relationships with these parents and guardians, and also with all families in your constituency. The more parents and guardians you are able to draw into your circle of trust, the more successful your inclusion program will be.

Building Trust with Parents and Guardians of Students on the Spectrum

As a parent, I'm sure I've gotten indignant when I felt a teacher was not challenging my son enough, and I'm sure I've also expressed anxiety when I felt a teacher was minimizing the extent of his challenges. As educators, we must remain keenly and consistently aware that these parents are engaged in various degrees of struggle, and that these kinds of conversations are deeply and emotionally loaded for them.

Due to the challenges these parents and guardians have faced along the road to your office, and due to their experience pushing against systems to get the supports their child needs, they may show up in your office in full fighting mode. Or they may arrive committed to the idea that only they know what their child needs. They may come with one or more chips on their shoulder, as described previously. Wherever they are, know that they have taken an arduous journey to get to this point and they are giving you whatever they've got left. Your goal is to meet these parents and guardians where they are with understanding and empathy, and to bridge the gaps to establish a productive and trusting collaboration. With that in mind, let's look at some practical strategies for providing support.

Respect the Struggle

The overarching principle when working with families of students on the spectrum is to give them the benefit of the doubt. When you find students showing up to school in clothes that are inappropriate for the weather, eating cold spaghetti with their fingers in the cafeteria, or bringing in homework completed in purple magic marker, don't go straight to "bad parenting." Again, don't be quick to judge. Instead, assume this: The parents did everything they could, but the student's rigidity got in the way. Or a meltdown over a misplaced Minion got in the way. Or any of a thousand possible stressors triggered the behavior, and the raw necessity of just getting through the day by whatever means necessary got in the way. Many, many parenting goals fall by the wayside when make-or-break issues intervene. Whenever you're called upon to address issues of concern, start there. Really.

Share Your Process

It is critical that educators *explain* to parents and guardians why they will or will not implement certain adaptations in the classroom. Following from the example earlier in this chapter, we need to explain to Rahul's parents that no teacher will be able to allow one student to make all the choices in the classroom and go first every time, the way Rahul does at home. We need to *explain* that school represents the "real world" in which all children will have to function one day to the best of their ability. School is also about promoting growth and development, and that means stretching children ever so gently out of their comfort zones. Let parents know that at school we do our best to *stretch* students without *stressing* them—an important distinction that needs to be made clear.

It is also critical that, at the same time, educators actively acknowledge that the family's adaptations may be lifesavers at home. Resist assuming that parents are enabling their kids by accommodating them in the ways that they are. What parents are doing is not enabling; it's called *survival.* Consider just how bad things must have gotten at home before a policy like letting one child make all the choices for the family could have developed. That's a kind of *behavioral drift.* It's not a decision any parent would make happily; it just develops gradually over time, in this case, due to necessity and desperation.

Meanwhile, it's important to decode the message parents and guardians are conveying when they put up these red flags and request adaptations that may not be suited to the school setting: this child is likely to act out in a dangerous or disruptive way when stressed. That is valuable information! Rather than dismiss the parents' expectation of class adaptations as unrealistic or overzealous, be grateful for the warning. Explain specifically to parents and guardians that teachers cannot be asked or expected to implement the same adaptations that have been made at home, and why. But also let them know that you are appreciative of the cautionary information and that you will use it to work with the teachers to devise creative solutions that will allow Rahul to feel safe and calm. Use the information you've been given to inform your teachers and staff that it's important for Rahul to feel he has some degree of choice or control of a situation, and let that information guide the preventive strategies implemented in the classroom. Perhaps Rahul can read the morning announcements, take attendance, pass out the equipment, choose his own workstation or his own calculator, or have other activities built into his day that enable him to feel he has a measure of control, while still preserving the rights of all of the other students to participate in choosing activities and to go first.

Focus on Student Strengths

As mentioned earlier, it's important to be mindful of the fact that most of these parents and guardians have received far more than their share of bad news from school. The world often offers these kids and their parents a steady stream of negative feedback, failure, impatience, and social rejection. In many cases, it's hard not to focus on the flagrant challenges and provocative behaviors these students present. Meetings of special ed teams, and the resultant IEPs and 504 plans, focus on challenges, not on strengths. It would be easy for parents and guardians to believe that at school, their child has been reduced to a stapled packet of deficits.

Similarly, bear in mind that attending behavior meetings—even positive, proactive ones—is something few parents of students on the spectrum enjoy doing. They'd much rather attend a different kind of school event—the kinds other parents get to attend, like an honor society induction or a varsity soccer match.

It's up to us, as education leaders, to focus on strengths. These may not always be easy to find, but if you can't find them, look harder. Praise Maya's honesty, call Tito out for his reliability, celebrate Rachel's schedule-following skills, commend Sean's command of dates and time. Presenting strengths first does more than foster a positive relationship and warm the hearts of parents who have been struggling. Leading with strengths also demonstrates that you see students as more than their challenges, that you see and value the whole child as a vital member of your school community.

This is not merely the suggestion of a new approach; it's the suggestion of a new attitude. Say it and mean it. Your genuine investment in and recognition of their whole child will help parents and guardians to let down their defenses and will bolster their ability to hear and accept any concerns you need to present.

Honor Different Kinds of Expertise

Educators and parents bring different kinds of wisdom to the picture of the whole child. Parents are the historical and holistic experts. They know every trigger, every single preemptive or responsive intervention that has helped, and every single highly touted intervention that has made things worse. They can see a meltdown coming a mile away. They know it all too well. They know.

Honor that. You can't possibly educate the whole child without taking the time to learn from the family. Listen, learn, and respect how far they've come.

However, it's important for all involved parties to remember that families and educators see children in different contexts. As noted earlier, students can be very different beings at school than they are at home. So even as you respect, validate, and appreciate the fact that parents and guardians know their child best at home, also let them know that you and your teachers offer a different kind of expertise: you know their child best *at school*. And your teachers' specialty is knowing how to teach a whole classroom of diverse students.

Pooling this respective wisdom is the way to build a truly collaborative brain trust. Tell parents that you welcome their perspectives and that you hope they will welcome yours, too. Sending home a questionnaire like the one in Figure 8.2 gives families the opportunity to share their hard-won wisdom. It signals to them that you're eager to collaborate and that you respect them as partners in this process. And, of course, the information you get back will give teachers a leg up in their work.

Figure 8.2: Sample Family Questionnaire

Dear Families,

Please fill out this questionnaire and return it to me by_____ .

Thank you for your support!

Child's name:_____ Nickname?_____

Parent(s)/Guardian(s):_____

Siblings (names and ages):   Parent/Guardian phone numbers:

_____ _____ ☐ work_____

_____ _____ ☐ home_____

_____ _____ ☐ mobile_____

                          ☐ mobile_____

Parent/Guardian e-mail   How do you prefer to be contacted?
address(es):
                          ☐ e-mail
_____
                          ☐ text
_____
                          ☐ phone
_____
                          If phone, what are the best times for
_____   me to call?_____

What are your child's specific strengths and/or special interests?

What academic subject does your child find most challenging?

What other aspects of the school day or routine (taking turns, listening, transitions, etc.) does your child find most challenging?

What kinds of situations make your child anxious or upset? How does he/she/they tend to react?

What comforts your child when he/she/they are anxious or upset? What makes things worse?

Please share any specific goals, hopes, or dreams you have for your child this year (social, emotional, academic, etc.):

Are there any other concerns or issues you would like me to know about or to watch out for?

Thank you! I look forward to working with you and your child this year.

_____

[Teacher signature and contact information]

Note: This form is available for download at www.ascd.org/ASCD/pdf/books/BorosonResources.pdf and at http://barbaraboroson.com/FamilyQuestionnaire.pdf

Communicate with Intention

Oh, the dreaded "call from school." Parents of students on the spectrum are used to carrying their phone everywhere they go during the school day—including into meetings at work, into the bathroom at home, and everywhere in between.

Because they will likely see the phone number of the school on their phone screen before they pick up, expect them to be on edge before you even say a word. *Was my child beaten up? Did he run away? Did he have a meltdown?* These are all reasonable fears for parents of students on the spectrum. So, let the first words out of your mouth be these: "Everything is OK."

Remember, too, that when parents get a call from the school about a behavior situation, they assume they are being asked to *do something about it.* Even if you describe an incident that you have handled capably and completely, and you report to parents that the student is now calm and all is well, parents may still assume—simply by virtue of the fact that you are calling—that you are putting the ball in their court. In these situations, a student may receive consequences at home for something that was already dealt with, cleared up, and put to rest at school. Here are two key ways to keep the channels of communication open.

Be specific about the *purpose* of your call. Are you calling to express concern about the child's well-being? Are you calling to keep parents in a planning or progress loop? To follow up with them on an ongoing situation or alert them to an escalating situation? To inform them of an incident? You might start the call like this: *Hello, Mr. DelGado. Everything is OK. I'm calling to tell you that x happened today.* Then describe the incident or situation before sharing your expectations from the call.

Be specific about the *expectations* from your call. Make sure you wrap up the call by stating what you hope will happen next. Are you letting them know about an incident so that they can give the child some extra love and support at home tonight— and not additional scolding or consequences? Do you want them to discuss the incident with their child (so that the child knows that school and home are connected and on the same page)? Do you believe that the child has learned from the experience and that no further consequences need to be enacted at home? If so, *say that specifically.* You might end the call with something like this: *I called only because I wanted you to know about it—not to get Caden in trouble at home. The situation was handled completely at school and it's over and done now. Please don't use any consequences—we* *took care of all of that at school. If you would like to discuss it with him and review better strategies for the future—great. But it was a rough day for Caden. What we think he needs mainly tonight is your loving support.*

Addressing Inclusion Concerns with Parents and Guardians of Students on the Spectrum

As a spokesperson for your inclusive school or district, you may be called upon to represent inclusion to a community of parents and guardians. Your audience runs the gamut from parents and guardians of students on the spectrum who may have very varied expectations for their children's education, to those who do not have kids with special needs and suffer egregious misconceptions about inclusion. In order to make the case for inclusive education and inclusion classrooms with confidence and conviction, you will need to be able to present and represent the ways in which your program serves all students well and enriches everyone's education experience.

Setting an Inclusive Tone:
The Dangers of Being Disability-Blind

Upon hearing about my work as an autism education consultant, one young teacher boasted to me, "I treat every student the same. I don't care whether they have autism or Down syndrome or no legs. I treat them all the same."

I know she meant well, but her comments made me cringe. These subgroups of students are certainly *not* the same—nor are the individual students within these subgroups the same; a policy that treats them as though they are the same provides none of them with what they need. This teacher's approach is reminiscent of color-blind race theory. The idea of not noticing differences relates to an abstract, idealized notion of equality that overlooks important and valuable differences. Undifferentiated ideas of equality often underlie efforts to make all people fit into a single construct of personhood, which is, in fact, the opposite of inclusive, differentiated thinking.

The work you and your staff do to forge open and trusting collaborative relationships with parents and guardians of students on the spectrum will have a powerful effect on bolstering your school's inclusion efforts. We've already looked at some of the steps you can take to connect to these parents. Now let's consider ways to move that collaboration forward to boost knowledge and acceptance of inclusion.

"Nothing to See Here"

Some parents and guardians will be 100 percent on board with their child's placement in an inclusion classroom from the outset. They believe their child on the spectrum should have an educational experience that is exactly the same as every other child's—not only equal access, but *identical* access. These parents or guardians may resist or even refuse modifications or accommodations that they fear might coddle their child or make their child look or feel different from the other students.

Although educators know that modifications and accommodations can be critical factors in the ability of students to be successful, parents may not realize that. When this is the case, explain to parents and guardians that it is the modifications and accommodations themselves that allow their child to succeed and to blend in with their peers. For example, parents may refuse to have their child sit on a bumpy cushion in class because "that's not what the other kids do." Explain to these parents that the bumpy cushion would enable their child to sit still, which would enable her to focus on lessons, which would enable her to participate in the lessons and in the follow-up group activities. Without the bumpy cushion, she has been unable to sit still, entire lessons have passed her by, and she has become disruptive during lessons, calling much more negative attention to herself than the bumpy cushion would. Moreover, because she has been unable to participate in the lessons, she has been incapable of contributing in the group activities, and so has been excluded from the social connections that develop during the group work. Her route to success depends on the modification.

"Better Safe Than Sorry"

On the other hand, some parents fear that an inclusion classroom will be "too much" for their vulnerable children. Indeed, this "least restrictive environment" may not be a place of ease and comfort for students on the spectrum; it is more likely to be a place of supported challenge. These parents and guardians are keenly aware of just how far their kids have come. They are also acutely, painfully aware of the precariousness of this relative success.

Inclusion Classrooms Are Not for Everyone

As you go around extolling the virtues of inclusive education, keep front of mind the fact that while inclusive education is for everyone, placement in an inclusion classroom is not suitable for every student. As described in Chapter 1, some students have special needs that are too difficult for teachers to address in this minimally restricted classroom, despite its many differentiated supports. Students who cannot cope in a large physical space with as many as 20 or more people in it, or whose behaviors are dysregulated enough to become a barrier to learning for others, or who require an entirely specialized and alternative curriculum should not, generally, be placed in an inclusion classroom.

This is important information to share with all parents and guardians. Parents and guardians of students on the spectrum need the assurance that your special education team places children in an inclusion classroom only after careful consideration and completion of a multistep evaluation process.

Parents and guardians of students who do not have disabilities will be reassured to know that not all students with special needs are eligible for placement in inclusion classrooms, and that there is a standard for inclusion. It will help them to know that the school's intention is to place in inclusion classrooms only those students whose special needs are not expected to be a barrier for learning for their classmates.

That being said, an inclusive school welcomes and accommodates every single student at schoolwide events and activities to the greatest extent possible, regardless of their class placement. That way, everyone is, indeed, included.

Try not to disdain or dismiss questions, concerns, and qualms as the hovering worries of helicopter parents. Do these parents worry? You bet they do. But they have much to worry about. Real practical and emotional challenges abound for parents and guardians of kids on the spectrum. Given the extreme shutdowns, breakdowns, and meltdowns many of these families have lived through, and the significant setbacks that came as a result, these parents have very good reason to be anxious about their children getting in over their heads. They know exactly how bad things will get and how devastating a setback it will be if their children are not protected from their most combustive triggers. That's why some parents and guardians ask for more safeguards and program adaptations than you may feel are necessary or reasonable.

Assure these parents and guardians that you and your teachers have ways of collecting data to help determine which supports are still needed and which ones can be carefully and mindfully faded. Reiterate that students may function very differently at school than they do at home. And remind them that we all share the goal of gradually moving these children toward independence, one supported step at a time.

Addressing Concerns with Parents and Guardians of Neurotypical Students

Much of the resistance to inclusion that you encounter in your school or district is likely to come from parents and guardians of typically developing students. Generally, their concerns come from the same place that most parental concern comes from: wanting the best for their children. In this case, it's often expressed as a fear that being in an inclusion classroom will cause their child to miss opportunities or be negatively affected in some way.

When parents and guardians are first exposed to the concept of inclusion, they usually hear that it's a program where students with special needs are included in "regular" classes. This oversimplification sets off a bit of a FOLO panic (fear of losing out): *How can a single gen ed teacher manage a whole classroom of students that includes students with special needs? How is that not going to take something away from the "regular" kids? My child has needs, too! My child deserves a fair share of the teacher's attention. I want my child in a "normal" class.*

These are understandable concerns. The thing is, for the most part, they are based on inaccurate assumptions. What manifests from parents as FOLO is actually FOTU (fear of the unknown), because parents and guardians of typically developing students are rarely provided much actual information about inclusion.

Often, because administrators and teachers are being careful not to violate the confidentiality of families of students with special needs, important facts about inclusion become an inadvertently guarded secret. But families of neurotypical students are absolutely affected by inclusion and need to be educated about it right alongside everyone else. The more they perceive a secret, the more FOTU they feel.

In order to create and maintain a successful inclusive program, we need buy-in from all involved parties: administrators, general ed teachers, special ed teachers, special area teachers, related service providers, building and bus staff . . . and all parents and guardians in the school community. In a bit of a catch-22, however, it can be difficult to get buy-in if you don't already have a successful inclusive program and therefore cannot speak confidently about it. Here are some guiding principles to help arm you with ideas and information that will promote inclusion enthusiasm and will, in turn, bolster the success of your program.

Inclusive Education Is for All Students

Our classrooms include students of diverse races, religions, cultures, nationalities, and orientations. There are students just learning the language, students of fluid or transitioning genders, students who need glasses or hearing aids or who use wheelchairs, students who come from peaceful homes, and students who come from chaotic or violent homes. There are students with differing academic abilities, kinds of social skills, sensory reactions, and behavioral styles. While I'm not suggesting that these are all *neutral* differences in the classroom, I *am* suggesting that they are *natural* differences in the classroom—as natural as anywhere else in life.

All this is to say that inclusive education is not just for students with disabilities or others with learning challenges; it's for all students. As stated above, all students in the building should be included in as many schoolwide activities and events as possible, to the greatest extent possible. Find differentiated ways to make it happen.

Moreover, discussion of inclusion classrooms should not be relegated to "special ed PTA" meetings. Consider working with PTA leaders to schedule informational meetings about inclusion geared toward all parents and guardians. There's nothing to hide. Shout it from the rooftops.

Inclusive Education as Best Practice

Inclusion classrooms are the perfect lab for a school's social-emotional learning (SEL) curriculum. More and more parents are buying into the importance of SEL skills for their children's long-term success. Help them to recognize that inclusion classrooms are microcosms of the real world. Through inclusive experiences, all children learn and practice ways of getting along with people who are different from themselves. They learn to help those who need help, and they learn to learn from those who experience the world differently. This sets them up with broad interpersonal understandings and interactional skills for careers in our new global society.

Jumping in with Both Feet

Nevertheless, many parents and guardians of children who do not have special education needs remain skeptical and resistant to having their kids included in inclusion, assuming that their children will suffer academically.

A major factor in determining how inclusion classrooms are received in your school or district relates to how they are represented. The devil is in the details, which, although they may seem insignificant to you, can send powerful messages to students and to parents about your commitment to inclusion and the teachers' commitment to creating a seamlessly inclusive, team-taught environment that benefits everyone.

Back up your words by following through on important signifiers that illustrate your commitment to inclusion. In co-taught classrooms, all students are assigned to both teachers; both teachers' names appear on the classroom door, the syllabus, grade reports, and all communications to parents; and both teachers attend and participate in parent-teacher conferences for all students in the class.

Figure 8.3 is a reproducible and distributable Myths and Facts guide that clarifies common misconceptions about inclusion for all families. Please use this information to help spread the word, advance the mission, and facilitate a program that is mutually supportive, seamlessly equitable, and exemplary of best-practice inclusive education that benefits all students.

● ▲ ◆ ◀ ■

This book started off by acknowledging that teaching students who are on the autism spectrum makes teaching harder. Facilitating an environment that includes their parents and guardians as partners may sound like an even more daunting proposition. But you and your teachers will find that as the entire community settles into and buys into inclusion, teaching and leading in an inclusive environment will become not only easier but infinitely more rewarding.

Figure 8.3: Inclusion Myths and Facts

INCLUSION MYTHS *and* FACTS

Inclusive education is the general practice of educating many kinds of learners and meeting the needs of all. An inclusion classroom, more specifically, is a specially designed class that brings together typical students and students who have special needs, providing a wide array of support and enrichment opportunities that are differentiated to benefit every student in the class, as described below.

MYTH	FACT
Inclusion classrooms are only for students who have special needs.	Most students in an inclusion classroom do not have special needs. Studies have shown that students with *and* without special needs benefit academically and socially from placement together in an inclusion classroom. Students who *do not* have special needs benefit from the extra opportunities for enrichment available in a classroom with two teachers. Students who *do* have special needs benefit from being less isolated and having access to more opportunities for socialization and learning. All students in the room benefit from being part of this diverse, creative, and stimulating classroom community.
Inclusion means that the district is tossing students who have special needs into "regular" classrooms to save money.	Inclusion classrooms are not just "regular" classrooms—they're better! Inclusion classrooms provide two credentialed teachers who work as a team to provide a variety of exciting learning opportunities. A tremendous amount of training, planning, and ongoing collaboration between the two teachers goes into creating and maintaining a learning environment that's optimal for everyone in it. No one is "tossed" into an inclusion class; students are selected for it.
Having kids with special needs in the classroom will take too much of the teachers' time away from the typically developing kids.	Inclusion teachers are trained to use a teaching method called *differentiation*. Based on the fact that no two learners are the same, differentiation guides teachers to adapt the delivery of the curriculum to best meet the needs of every single student rather than forcing every student to adapt to a rigid, one-size-fits-all curriculum. Differentiation leads to creative opportunities for both individualized support and enrichment.

Continued ▶

Figure 8.3: Inclusion Myths and Facts (*continued*)

MYTH	FACT
Some kids who have special needs can be very disruptive or require a lot of support. They will be too difficult for the teachers to handle in an inclusion classroom.	It's true that inclusion is not the best fit for every student. That's why students who have special needs are not automatically placed in inclusion classrooms. Very careful consideration is given to ensure that the inclusion classroom, with its full size and grade-level curriculum, will be best suited to each student's needs. If it is determined that a student's placement in an inclusion classroom would constitute a barrier to learning for *any* students in the room, then an alternative classroom setting is recommended for that student.
The behavior of students with special needs will be a bad influence or will distract other students.	Every classroom of children has its share of undesirable behavior. If students who have special needs do act out, their behavior is usually a way of communicating distress. Most inclusion teachers are expert at decoding those behaviors and addressing the cause of the distress in ways that resolve the behavior quickly and also prevent it from recurring. You may see students wearing noise-cancelling headphones or using assistive technology. Tools like these help prevent acting out behavior. As in all classrooms, positive behaviors are clearly reinforced for all students.
Students with special needs who are placed in self-contained special ed classes instead of inclusion classrooms will be left out of schoolwide activities or events.	Inclusive education is a concept that extends beyond the walls of the classroom to ensure that the entire school is a welcoming place for every student. Children with special needs who are not placed in inclusion classrooms are still absolutely part of the inclusive school community. Schoolwide events and activities will be differentiated to the greatest extent possible so that all members of the school community can participate.
Students who don't have special needs are placed in inclusion classrooms because the school is trying to sneak them into special education.	There is no trickery, deception, or spin involved in inclusion. Students who do not have special needs may be placed in an inclusion class because they have demonstrated strong social skills or have shown that they would benefit from individualized enrichment that goes beyond the standard curriculum. Others may present with unique talents that warrant opportunities to learn through creative expression and exploration. Differentiated inclusion classrooms are generally able to allow for more individualized enrichment and support than many other kinds of classrooms can, all while pursuing grade-level curriculum.
Some students with special needs are allowed to do things other students are not allowed to do, like chew gum or get more time for tests. That's not right. Everything should be equal in the classroom.	It's true that, in some circumstances, certain students will be allowed to engage in activities or opportunities that others will not. Treating every student equally would mean making sure every child gets exactly the same thing, which actually goes against the goals of a differentiated inclusion classroom. Instead of giving every student the same thing, inclusion classrooms give every student what he, she, or they need. It is better than equal; it is fair.

Note: This form is available for download at www.ascd.org/ASCD/pdf/books/BorosonResources.pdf and also at http://barbaraborson.com/InclusionMyths-Facts.pdf

Conclusion

In this era of inclusive education, most of our classrooms, schools, and districts are more heterogeneous than they used to be. That means that as education leaders, we need to think far outside the box. In fact, maybe we should just bust right out of the box. Maybe there is no more box. Today, we need to use ourselves differently and do our best to view our schools and districts through a multifocal lens. As described throughout this book, our inclusive programs include individuals who may experience school through the lens of anxiety, the lens of sensory reactivity, the lens of social naiveté. Others experience school through the lens of dyslexia, dysgraphia, or vision impairment, or through Down syndrome, cerebral palsy, or spina bifida. Still others through poverty, cultural difference, or the challenge of English language acquisition.

Today, we need to be open enough, flexible enough, inclusive enough to make our programs work for *everyone*. Consider the many traditions that have become legendary milestones in the culture of your district—whether it's the senior prom, the homecoming varsity football game, the annual 8th grade camping trip, the 5th grade science fair, the 2nd grade poetry slam, or the kindergarten Halloween parade. With absolutely all the best intentions, educators tend to glorify these special events with enthusiastic language like, "*Everybody* always has a great time!" and "You'll love this activity. *Everyone* does."

My son was 3 years old the first time my family learned that "everyone" didn't include us. That sobering message is reiterated all the time, and even after 21 years, it still makes us feel overlooked, irrelevant, and excluded. There's "everyone," and then there's us—our family with autism.

As you come to the end of this book, I hope you will step back and look at your program and all that it entails from an all-access perspective. Reimagine experiences and activities with an eye toward making them accessible to all—not only in terms of ramps and elevators but also in terms of sound, light, structure, and social facilitation. Look closely for other potential access-blockers, such as whether participation in certain activities would necessitate fluency in English; the removal of head coverings or other items of religious apparel; or the consumption of food that is off-limits or dangerous to some due to allergies, medical restrictions, or religious or cultural mores. Build in creative solutions that allow for and inspire a variety of ways to partake in the learning and the fun.

If your program is going to be truly inclusive, let your language and your efforts reflect that diverse spirit. The mantra of inclusion is not *We are one;* it's *We are all different, and we love it that way.*

Let's set our sights on a time when no conscious effort is needed to accept, welcome, teach, and play with students who are different; they'll just be there, woven throughout the fabric of all our classrooms and schools. As I pointed out in an article published in 2017, when we use the lens of neurodiversity to look at the classroom, we can see that "diverse learners do not dilute the dignity and integrity of a learning environment. Rather, diverse learners breathe energy, openness, and vitality into our classrooms and curriculum, so that for future generations, diversity will be mainstream, and appreciation of differences will be the one thing we all have in common" (Boroson, 2017, p. 23). Let's work together to make this vision a reality in every school and every district—and for every child.

Acknowledgments

I've been lucky to get to work with the creative and truly collaborative publishing team at ASCD who shepherded this book with such care: Stefani Roth, Genny Ostertag, Donald Ely, Keith Demmons, Jennifer Morgan, Laura Larson, Cynthia Landeen, Eddie Duff, and especially my editor and sister resister Katie Martin. Many thanks also to Carol Collins for getting it off the ground and Allison Scott for keeping it off the ground.

I'm grateful to the education professionals who generously contributed their wisdom and experience: Lisa Boerum, Laken Brooks, Shelley Chandler, Ellis Crasnow, Janet Ferone, Terry Ottina, Kelly Robinson, Carole Schaffan, Rachel Smith, and Lorraine Sobson.

Big thanks to my local union of unwitting short bus drivers: Ann Horowitz, Una Murray, Peggy O'Leary, and Katharine Page for keeping me going, and my reliably "lippy" friends Terry Dunn and Marla Levine for keeping me writing and laughing. Thanks to Ken Boroson, Linda Goodman, Bernie Boroson, Judy Stuart Boroson, and Helen Rutt for cheering me on. Love you.

Finally, thank you to Rosie, my stalwart writing companion, for faithfully reminding me to take breaks by slamming the computer shut on my hands. And most of all, love to Marty Boroson, Andrew Dodd, Sam Boroson Rutt, Leana Boroson Rutt, and Joe Rutt. You guys are my absolutely everything.

Appendix:
Fact & Tip Sheets for
Whole-School Support

Facts & Tips for Special Area Teachers

The information on this sheet will help you create a positive learning environment for students on the autism spectrum while they are with you. Thanks for your willingness to learn about and support them!

Students who are on the autism spectrum are quirky, endearing kids who struggle with a wide range of challenges in any or all of the following areas:

Anxiety: Students on the spectrum often have limited coping skills, which can lead to extreme anxiety in unfamiliar situations. They depend heavily on routines and structure, and may cling to certain objects or repetitive interests to help them feel safe.

✔ Ask the teacher to help you prepare a visual schedule to create predictability and reduce anxiety.

Rigidity: Students on the spectrum tend to be rigid rule followers. Rules make life more manageable and predictable. *These students very much want to follow the rules but may not understand exactly what the rules are or what they imply.* This same rigidity means these students may get extremely agitated when rules are broken or when something unexpected happens.

✔ Use concrete and specific language. Try to make your expectations as clear as possible.

Communication: Many of these students express themselves in unusual ways or have a hard time making their thoughts and needs known. They may also have difficulty understanding your words.

✔ Remember that making conversation is a developing skill. Be patient and supportive.

Socialization: These students struggle socially. Interactions may be awkward, one-sided, or nonexistent. Be aware that social challenges make these students very vulnerable to being bullied.

✔ Keep a watchful and protective eye out for provocation, bullying, teasing, or other disrespectful treatment by peers.

Sensation: Most students on the autism spectrum take in far too much or far too little sensory input. Hand-flapping, rocking, and similar behaviors are related to sensory challenges.

✔ Adapt the sensory environment based on individual needs and teacher input. *Offer options whenever possible.*

Behavior: *All behavior is a form of communication.* Difficult behaviors indicate that something is wrong. Chances are, a behavioral problem is the result of one of the challenges described above.

✔ When students on the autism spectrum misbehave, they need help— not consequences.

Inside/Outside: Some students on the autism spectrum demonstrate obvious, *external* challenges: They may flick their fingers or talk endlessly about a single topic.

✔ Don't *underestimate* these students; they may have lots of clever, creative ideas going on inside.

Other students are primarily affected by *internal* challenges: They may appear typical.

✔ Don't *overestimate* these students; they may struggle intensely with many challenges that can't readily be seen.

Know Your Student

- Don't reinvent the wheel! Talk with the classroom teacher or case manager to find out what your student's special interests are, how best to engage them, what tends to set a student off, and what makes things better.

- Read the IEP to find out more about the challenges this student faces and what goals have been set.

- Attend team meetings to learn about current stressors and new strategies. If you can't get there, ask for a summary of the discussion and recommendations.

Flip the page for specific suggestions!

Facts & Tips for Special Area Teachers, cont.

Perspectives on Art

Break the Mold: Sensory challenges abound in the art room, any of which may be unbearable: the feel of fingerpaint, glue, clay, charcoal, papier maché, or oil pastels; the smell of paints, markers, plaster, pottery dust; the sound of markers, Styrofoam, or wood sanders. Offer choices of medium.

Paint with a Broad Brush: Be aware that fine motor and visual-motor challenges may cause students to grip and press on art implements so hard that they tear the paper or so lightly that their work is illegible. Allow use of various implements and accept alternate outcomes.

Realism Versus Impressionism: Some students on the autism spectrum struggle to differentiate colors, shapes, and other detailed elements of pictures, such as subject versus shadow and figure versus ground. Accept general impressions if details are elusive.

> ## Elaborating on Collaborating
>
> Group work is a special challenge for students on the spectrum. Here's how you can maximize success:
>
> - Give a whole-class lesson on group-work skills including flexibility, negotiation, compromise, tolerating mistakes, problem solving, and recognizing when and how to get help.
> - Choose group-mates mindfully.
> - Create structure by assigning roles that are suited to individual strengths. Consider positions like media manager, art critic, music critic, efficiency expert, or fact-checker.

Music Notes

Scale It Back: The sounds of some instruments may be painful to some kids—sometimes. Watch the volume. Headphones, earplugs, and area rugs are effective at making the sound and acoustics manageable for students on the autism spectrum.

Tune In: Sensory discrimination challenges may prevent some students from distinguishing among musical tones and rhyming sounds. Allow flexible types of musical interpretation.

Drum Up Alternatives: Consider fine motor, oral motor, and visual-motor challenges when students play or read music. Offer instruments that require less or different types of coordination.

Library Reference

Brave New World: Moving abruptly from the noisy hallway into the silent library can be very challenging for students on the autism spectrum. Help them shift gears by providing gentle support and allowing them time to make the adjustment.

Great Expectations: Among many students on the spectrum, decoding is far stronger than comprehension. Look for books that pair age-level content with simpler text. Graphic novels can be very accessible to students on the spectrum.

A Series of Fortunate Events: Engagement is one of the greatest obstacles in getting students on the spectrum to read. Take the time to introduce students to a series. Once your student is acquainted with Violet, Claude, Sunny, and Count Olaf (or with Harry, Ron, and Hermione), those characters provide a thread of familiarity that can open up whole new worlds.

Classroom Teacher Notes:

_____

_____

_____

For more information, touch base with the classroom teacher or principal (or browse through *Autism Spectrum Disorder in the Inclusive Classroom*).

Facts & Tips for
Classroom Paraprofessionals

The information on this sheet will help you play a positive role in the school experience of students on the autism spectrum. Thank you for your willingness to learn about and support these kids!

Students who are on the autism spectrum are quirky, endearing kids who struggle with a wide range of challenges in any or all of the following areas:

Anxiety: Students on the spectrum often have limited coping skills, which can lead to extreme anxiety in unfamiliar situations. Visual schedules, routines, structure, and repetitive interests help them feel safe. *Be patient and supportive.* Life on the autism spectrum can be overwhelming. That's why you're here.

Rigidity: Students on the spectrum tend to be rigid rule followers. Rules help make life feel more manageable and predictable. *These students very much want to follow the rules but may not understand exactly what the rules are or what they imply.* This same rigidity means these students may get extremely agitated when rules are broken or when something unexpected happens.

Communication: Many of these students express themselves in unusual ways or have a hard time making their thoughts and needs known. They may also have difficulty understanding your words. Use visual symbols and concrete, specific language to make communication as clear as possible.

Socialization: These students struggle to make friends. Interactions may be awkward, one-sided, or nonexistent. Be aware that social challenges make these students very vulnerable to bullying. Keep a watchful and protective eye out for provocation, teasing, or other disrespectful treatment by peers. Many people don't see past the challenges; help others recognize your student's fabulousness!

Sensation: Most students on the spectrum take in far too much or far too little sensory input. Hand-flapping, rocking, and similar behaviors are necessary to help students cope with their sensory challenges. When they feel overwhelmed, be calm and reassuring. Loud, angry voices will make things worse, not better.

Inside/Outside: Some students on the spectrum demonstrate obvious, *external* challenges: They may flick their fingers or talk endlessly about a single topic. Don't *underestimate* these students; they may have lots of clever, creative ideas going on inside. Other students are primarily affected by *internal* challenges: They may appear typical. Don't *overestimate* these students; they may struggle intensely with many challenges that can't readily be seen.

Behavior: *All behavior is a form of communication.* Difficult behaviors indicate that something is wrong. When students on the autism spectrum misbehave, they need help—not consequences. Be a detective. Look for patterns and warning signs so that you can ease the situations that trigger strong reactions before difficult behaviors erupt.

For guidance on offering meaningful one-on-one support in the classroom, flip the page.

Facts & Tips for Classroom Paraprofessionalss, *cont.*

Support for Supporters

On the Front Lines: You are on the front lines of challenging behavior. There will be moments when it is hard for you to stay calm and patient—but it's crucial that you remain professional. When a student loses control, try not to take her words or behaviors personally. She cannot control herself or learn independently yet. Remember that impulsivity is *part of her disability.* Your student needs to be guided to learn more positive ways of functioning in the classroom and beyond. Be prepared to repeat yourself. This kind of learning takes time.

What's Up: While the teacher must attend to the needs of many students, you have a uniquely up-close-and-personal perspective to see details the teacher cannot. When you notice small signs of progress or new areas of concern, offer to share them with the classroom teacher.

Backing Off: *The best help you can provide is to gently guide your student toward independence.* Be on the lookout for hot spots—those times when he needs you to help him manage a challenging situation. But also look for times when you can fade your support and let him do his thing, independently.

Don't worry about "appearing" busy: The teacher and principal understand that you don't need to be interacting every moment in order to be doing your job well. This doesn't mean you can zone out. Instead, you need to remain fully engaged and attentive to your student, even from a distance.

Keeping It on the D.L.: Be aware that all personal information about specific students must, by law, be kept strictly confidential. You may not share *any* personal information about students with other building staff, bus drivers, students, other parents, or with your friends and family. Don't even share the *name* of the student to whom you are assigned.

You can discuss this student only with other school professionals who work with him or her, such as the classroom teacher, principal, or therapists. But take care that such conversations are not overheard by others.

The Rules of Cool: Needing a 1:1 aide can be a tremendous source of embarrassment, especially in upper elementary, middle, and high school. Do your best not to make your student feel singled out and different. Keep your interventions discreet and low key, give him a little space when possible, and offer help to other students when you are available.

Classroom Teacher Notes:

_____

_____

_____

_____

_____

For more information, touch base with the classroom teacher or principal (or browse through *Autism Spectrum Disorder in the Inclusive Classroom*).

Facts & Tips for
Building Staff and Bus Staff

The information on this sheet will help you play a positive role in the entire school experience of students on the autism spectrum. Thank you for your willingness to learn about and support these kids!

Students who are on the autism spectrum are quirky, endearing kids who struggle with a wide range of challenges in any or all of the following areas:

Anxiety: Students on the spectrum often have limited coping skills, which can lead to extreme anxiety in unfamiliar situations. They depend heavily on routines, structure, and repetitive interests to help them feel safe.

Rigidity: Students on the spectrum tend to be rigid rule followers. Rules help make life feel more manageable and predictable. *These students very much want to follow the rules but may not understand exactly what the rules are or what they imply.* This same rigidity means these students tend to get extremely agitated when rules are broken or when something unexpected happens.

Communication: Many of these students have a hard time making their thoughts and needs known clearly. They may also have difficulty understanding your words.

Socialization: These students rarely understand how to interact with others in socially expected ways. Conversation may be awkward, one-sided, or nonexistent. Be aware that social challenges make these students very vulnerable to bullying.

Sensation: Students on the autism spectrum often have sensory challenges. They may take in far too much or far too little sensory input. Hand-flapping, spinning, rocking, and similar behaviors are necessary to help students to cope with their sensory challenges.

Inside/Outside: Some students on the spectrum demonstrate many obvious *external* challenges: They may flick their fingers, have trouble speaking, or talk endlessly about a single obscure topic. Don't *underestimate* these students; they may have lots of clever, creative ideas going on inside. Other students are primarily affected by *internal* challenges: They may seem typical in appearance or in conversation. Don't *overestimate* these students; they may struggle intensely with cognitive, communicative, emotional, sensory, and other challenges that can't readily be seen.

Behavior: *All behavior is a form of communication.* Difficult behaviors tell you that something is wrong. When students who are on the spectrum misbehave, they need help—not consequences.

Here are some simple ways you can support these kids in your everyday interactions with them:

✔ Use concrete and specific language. Try to make your expectations as clear as possible.

✔ Be calm and reassuring. Loud, angry voices will make things worse, not better.

✔ Remember that making conversation is a developing skill. Be patient and supportive.

✔ Praise them for the skills they are doing well and remember that manners may not be a priority—yet.

✔ Keep a watchful and protective eye out for bullying or other disrespectful treatment by peers.

✔ Above all, be mindful of the enormous challenges these students face at every turn and help them feel safe and supported in our school.

Flip the page for specific suggestions in your area of the school community!

Facts & Tips for Building Staff and Bus Staff, cont.

Cafeteria Workers: The cafeteria is sensory chaos: Kids are shouting, chairs are scraping, smells are stewing. The lunch line presents new challenges every day, requiring quick thinking and decision making. The social pressure is intense. And it's all without the support of the teacher and the comfort of the classroom! Be patient and help students through this unrelentingly stressful experience.

Recess Monitors: The playground, which is supposed to be fun, can be a sensory and social nightmare for students on the spectrum. They may need help taking turns with equipment and understanding the rules of games. They often get teased, left out, or bullied, so they need close supervision when they are out among their peers. Keep in mind that you can't recognize bullying from a distance; keep a close eye and ear on peer interactions to be sure that everyone is OK.

School Nurse: The fragile equilibrium of students on the autism spectrum can be easily shattered. Some students have strong sensory reactions and feel discomfort very intensely, even if their symptoms may not seem so bad to you. They're not being hypochondriacs; trust that if they say something hurts, something hurts. But be aware that some students may find it very difficult to communicate clearly what hurts and in what way it hurts.

On the other hand, some students on the spectrum may be less aware of pain and discomfort than others. They can get badly injured but feel nothing. They need to be watched for fever, nausea, dizziness, internal bleeding, and other internal problems, especially following a fall or collision.

Office Staff: Know that it may be a significant achievement for students on the spectrum simply to leave the classroom on their own. Remembering the route to the office, and figuring out what to do when they get to you, may be all they can handle now. Congratulate them on a job well done, even if they don't greet you with a proper "Good morning."

Custodians: You are often the first responders when drinks spill or when vomit happens. These incidents are extremely upsetting to students on the spectrum because their rigid rules and expectations may have been accidentally and dramatically broken. Also keep in mind that some students have difficulty with motor coordination, which may make them especially clumsy. No matter what has happened, be gentle and reassuring and know that the incident is far more troubling to them than it is to you.

Bus Staff: The bus ride poses endless challenges for students on the autism spectrum. It's loud, it's crowded, it's a social minefield, and it's an anxious transitional time between one comfort zone (home) and another (school). You cannot be available to support sensory challenges and social skills while you're driving, but you can encourage vulnerable students to sit near you and allow them to wear earplugs or headphones if it helps them feel better.

> ## Keeping it on the D.L.
>
> Be aware that any information you receive about specific students must, by law, be kept strictly confidential. You may not share any personal information about students with other building staff, bus drivers, students, or with your friends and family.
>
> However, if you observe or are involved in an incident with a student, discuss it with the school personnel who work with a particular child— e.g., his or her teacher, the principal, or the student's aide. But take care that such conversations are not overheard by others.

Classroom Teacher Notes:

_____

_____

For more information, touch base with the classroom teacher or principal (or browse through *Autism Spectrum Disorder in the Inclusive Classroom*).

Facts & Tips for
PE Teachers and Coaches

The information on this sheet will help you create a positive learning environment for students on the autism spectrum while they are with you. Thanks for your willingness to learn about and support them!

Students who are on the autism spectrum are quirky, endearing kids who struggle with a wide range of challenges in any or all of the following areas:

Anxiety: Students on the spectrum often have limited coping skills, which can lead to extreme anxiety in unfamiliar situations. They depend heavily on routines and structure, and may cling to certain objects or repetitive interests to help them feel safe.
  - ✔ Ask the teacher to help you prepare a visual schedule to create predictability and reduce anxiety.

Rigidity: Students on the spectrum tend to be rigid rule followers. Rules make life more manageable and predictable. *These students very much want to follow the rules but may not understand exactly what the rules are or what they imply.* This same rigidity means these students may get extremely agitated when rules are broken or when something unexpected happens.
  - ✔ Use concrete and specific language to make your expectations as clear as possible.

Communication: Many of these students express themselves in unusual ways or have a hard time making their thoughts and needs known. They may also have difficulty understanding your words.
  - ✔ Remember that making conversation is a developing skill. Be patient and supportive.

Socialization: These students struggle socially. Interactions may be awkward, one-sided, or nonexistent. Be aware that social challenges make these students very vulnerable to being bullied.
  - ✔ Keep a watchful and protective eye out for provocation, bullying, teasing, or other disrespectful treatment by peers.

Sensation: Most students on the spectrum take in far too much or far too little sensory input. Hand-flapping, rocking, and similar behaviors are related to sensory challenges.
  - ✔ Adapt the sensory environment based on individual needs and teacher input. Offer options whenever possible.

Behavior: *All behavior is a form of communication.* Difficult behaviors indicate that something is wrong. Chances are, a behavioral problem is the result of one of the challenges described above.
  - ✔ When students on the spectrum misbehave, they need help—not consequences.

Inside/Outside: Some students on the autism spectrum demonstrate obvious, *external* challenges: They may flick their fingers or talk endlessly about a single topic.
  - ✔ Don't *underestimate* these students; they may have lots of clever, creative ideas going on inside.

Other students are primarily affected by *internal* challenges: They may appear typical.
  - ✔ Don't *overestimate* these students; they may struggle intensely with many challenges that can't readily be seen.

Flip the page for specific suggestions!

Facts & Tips for PE Teachers and Coaches, *cont.*

Overcoming Hurdles in PE Class

Take One for the Team: Being part of a team is a special challenge for students on the spectrum. Before breaking into teams, take a few minutes to conduct a whole-class lesson on teamwork. Review important skills like flexibility, patience, negotiation, compromise, tolerating mistakes, problem solving, and recognizing when and how to get help. Choose teammates kindly and mindfully. Create structure by offering positions that play to individual strengths, such as timekeeper, scorekeeper, equipment manager, efficiency expert, or sportscaster.

Run Interference: The sounds of pounding feet and skidding sneakers may be overwhelming to students on the spectrum. Look for signs of discomfort. Offer breaks or, *if necessary*, less intense ways of participating.

Par for the Course: Poor athletic performance may be due to challenges of gross motor, visual-motor, or hand-eye coordination; motor planning; focus; or auditory processing. Offer gentle guidance and optional activities that play to a student's skills.

Lay Out the Game Plan: Sit everyone down quietly to explain or review the rules of a new game. Comprehension will be up when noise and movement and other distractions are down. Also be aware that these students may not have been included in pick-up games in the neighborhood, so they may not know basic rules of common games.

Touch Base: In physical education, adrenaline flows and aggressive instincts surge. This is a socially vulnerable time for students on the autism spectrum. You can't see or hear bullying from the pitcher's mound. Move around the field, the dugout, or the court to listen and look closely for signs of trouble.

And They're Off: Some students on the spectrum have difficulty with balance and stability. Activities that require them to be off the ground or upside down, such as climbing, gymnastics, or yoga, may be dizzyingly disorienting. Be at the ready with extra support or alternative activities, if needed.

Foul! Students on the autism spectrum are rigid rule followers. They've been taught all their lives that it's never OK to push others or to grab a toy from someone else's hands. Suddenly, in competitive sports, *shoving*, *tackling*, and *stealing* are encouraged and celebrated. To kids on the spectrum, that's just WRONG. Teach them that here, in PE class, during specific games, it really is OK.

Classroom Teacher Notes:

_____

_____

_____

_____

Know Your Student

- Don't reinvent the wheel! Talk with the classroom teacher or case manager to find out what tends to set a student off and what makes things better.

- Read the IEP to find out more about the challenges this student faces and what goals have been set.

- Attend team meetings to learn about current stressors and new strategies. If you can't get there, ask for a summary of the discussion and recommendations.

For more information, touch base with the classroom teacher or principal (or browse through *Autism Spectrum Disorder in the Inclusive Classroom*).

Facts & Tips for Related Service Providers

The information on this sheet will help you create a supportive therapeutic environment for students on the autism spectrum during their time with you. Thank you for your willingness to learn about and support them!

Students who are on the autism spectrum are quirky, endearing kids who struggle with a wide range of challenges in any or all of the following areas:

Anxiety: Students on the spectrum often have limited coping skills, which can lead to extreme anxiety in unfamiliar situations. They depend on routines and structure and may cling to certain objects or repetitive interests to help them feel safe.

✔ Prepare a visual schedule for your sessions to create predictability and reduce anxiety. If necessary, carry a transition schedule with you to and from sessions. Ask teachers to share access to schedule-making resources with you.

Rigidity: Students on the spectrum tend to be rigid rule followers. Rules make life more manageable and predictable. *These students want to follow the rules but may not understand exactly what the rules are or what they imply.* This same rigidity means that these students may get extremely agitated when rules are broken or when something unexpected happens.

✔ Use concrete and specific language. Try to make your expectations as clear as possible.

Communication: Many of these students express themselves in unusual ways or have a hard time making their thoughts and needs known. They may also have difficulty understanding your words or instructions.

✔ Remember that making conversation is a developing skill. Supplement your words with visual prompts and plenty of patience.

Engagement: Students on the spectrum tend to be deeply focused on specialized areas of interest. This can prevent them from attending to or engaging in your lessons.

✔ To boost comfort and familiarity, let them practice new skills and strategies in the context of their special interests before expanding to other topics.

Sensation: Students on the spectrum often use repetitive, self-stimulatory behaviors ("stims"), like hand-flapping or rocking, to regulate an imbalance of sensation in their systems.

✔ Creating a calm, soothing therapeutic environment will reduce students' need to rely on stims. Do not try to prohibit stimming behaviors, as they are important coping mechanisms.

Behavior: *All behavior is a form of communication.* Difficult behaviors indicate that something is wrong. Chances are, a behavioral problem is the result of one of the challenges described above.

✔ Ask to be included in team meetings or to receive written summaries of them, so you can learn about relevant stressors and strategies. Remember that when students on the spectrum misbehave, they need help—not consequences.

Inside/Outside: Some students who are on the autism spectrum demonstrate obvious, *external* challenges: They may flick their fingers or talk endlessly about a single topic.

✔ Don't *underestimate* these students; they may have lots of clever, creative ideas going on inside.

Other students are primarily affected by *internal* challenges: They may appear typical.

✔ Don't *overestimate* these students; they may struggle intensely with many challenges that can't readily be seen.

Flip the page to find ideas for your discipline!

Facts & Tips for Related Service Providers, *cont.*

Speech & Language Therapy

That Sounds Familiar: Students on the spectrum often use scripting (i.e., reciting lines from movies, TV shows, commercials) to communicate. They also tend to perseverate on certain topics. Scripting and perseverating are ways of making conversation predictable. Provide and practice an array of expectable responses to varied conversational prompts that can be memorized and performed by rote.

Look Who's Talking: Students on the spectrum tend to communicate more effectively with adults than with peers because adult language tends to be more straightforward and predictable. Their interactions with you are not representative of their overall functioning. Be sure to obtain a clear sense of the challenges they encounter in all contexts.

Power Up: New augmentative and assistive communication devices and apps are being created all the time for minimally verbal or nonverbal students. These tools facilitate interaction and enhance motivation for students on the spectrum. Stay up to date with new technologies in this area.

Occupational and Physical Therapy

Common Sense: As many as 95 percent of students on the autism spectrum face sensory challenges. Be sure that IEP goals address sensory processing skills, and make sensory integration therapy a priority when working with these students.

Share Your Wisdom: OT and PT challenges have a significant effect on these students in the classroom. Share your wisdom and adaptive strategies, devices, and tools with classroom teachers, and champion the use of sensory spaces, rooms, and paths in your school.

Teach and Reteach: Many students on the spectrum have difficulty retaining new information and skills. Be patient if you need to teach, reteach, and practice the same skills many times before they are assimilated into cognitive memory or muscle memory.

Counseling

Whatever Works: Students on the spectrum may not be able to tell you what's on their mind or how they are feeling. Make good use of social stories, as well as aspects of play therapy, art therapy, and drama therapy techniques—at all ages—to facilitate communication and social learning.

Lunchtime Learning: Join forces with speech–language pathologists to offer ongoing social skill groups to students on the spectrum during lunch or after school—even if it's not mandated.

Buddy Up: Recruit typically developing students to volunteer as buddies in classrooms and hallways and during unstructured periods like lunch, recess, and study hall. Create an afterschool club to promote social interaction and build relationships between students on the spectrum and their typically developing peers.

Classroom Teacher Notes:

_____

_____

Generally Speaking...

Students on the autism spectrum have significant difficulty generalizing new skills from one setting to another. Here are some ways you can support their efforts:

- Be sure to let students know specifically that the goal is for them to use their new skills *everywhere*, not just in the therapy room.

- While small pull-out sessions may be necessary for focused skill instruction, try to add push-in support whenever and wherever possible to help these students apply their new skills in natural settings.

- Assign "homework" that requires students to practice their new skills at home, in the classroom, and out in the community.

- Let teachers and parents or guardians know what skills you are actively working on so that they can reinforce your directives across contexts.

References

Adelman, H., & Taylor, L. (2015). *Mental health in schools: Engaging learners, preventing problems, and improving schools*. Brattleboro, VT: Skyhorse Publishing.

American Academy of Pediatrics. (2018, July 24). *Vaccine safety: Examine the evidence*. Retrieved from https://www.healthychildren.org/English/safety-prevention/immunizations/Pages/Vaccine-Studies-Examine-the-Evidence.aspx

American Psychiatric Association. (1994). *Diagnostic and statistical manual of mental disorders* (4th ed.). Washington, DC: Author.

American Psychological Association. (2013). *Diagnostic and statistical manual of mental disorders* (5th ed.). Washington, DC: Author.

American Psychiatric Association. (2015). *APA dictionary of psychology* (2nd ed.). Washington, DC: Author.

Anderson, M. D. (2015, September 14). Will school-discipline reform actually change anything? *The Atlantic*. Retrieved from https://www.theatlantic.com/education/archive/2015/09/will-school-discipline-reform-actually-change-anything/405157/

Ashley, J., & Burke, K. (2010). *Implementing restorative justice: A guide for schools*. Chicago: Illinois Criminal Justice Information Authority.

AWAARE Collaboration. (n.d.) *Resources for school administrators*. Retrieved from https://awaare.nationalautismassociation.org/for-school-administrators/

Baio, J., Wiggins, L., Christensen, D. L., Maenner, M. J., Daniels, J., Warren, Z., . . . Dowling, N. F. (2018). Prevalence of autism spectrum disorder among children aged 8 years—Autism and Developmental Disabilities Monitoring Network, 11 sites, United States, 2014. *MMWR Surveillance Summary, 67* (No. SS-6), 1–23. doi: 10.15585/mmwr.ss6706a1

Bariso, J. (2018, September 9). There are actually 3 types of empathy. Here's how they differ—and how you can develop them all. Retrieved from https://www.inc.com/justin-bariso/there-are-actually-3-types-of-empathy-heres-how-they-differ-and-how-you-can-develop-them-all.html

Belisle, A. (2017, March 14). How response to intervention (RTI) became a national movement to support struggling learners [Blog post]. Retrieved from *Cisco Blogs at* https://blogs.cisco.com/csr/how-response-to-intervention-rti-became-a-national-movement-to-support-struggling-learners

Boroson, B. (2017, April). Inclusive education: Lessons from history. *Educational Leadership, 74*(7), 18–23.

Brewer, R., & Murphy, J. (2016, July 13). People with autism can read emotions, feel empathy. Retrieved from *Scientific American/Spectrum.* at https://www.scientificamerican.com/article/people-with-autism-can-read-emotions-feel-empathy1/

CASEL. (2018, October). *Connecting schoolwide SEL with other school-based frameworks.* Retrieved from https://schoolguide.casel.org/uploads/2019/01/SEL_MTSS-and-PBIS .pdf

CAST. (2018). *The UDL guidelines.* Retrieved from http://udlguidelines.cast.org

Demetriou, E. A., Lampit, A., Quintana, D. S., Naismith, S. L., Song, Y. J. C., Pye, J. E., Hickle, I., & Guastella, A. J. (2018). Autism spectrum disorders: A meta-analysis of executive function. *Molecular Psychiatry, 23,* 1198–1204.

Draper, S. (2012). *Out of my mind.* New York: Simon & Schuster.

Elder, J. (2005). *Different like me: My book of autism heroes.* London: Jessica Kingsley Publishers.

Frith, U. (1989). Autism and "theory of mind." In C. Gillberg (Ed.), *Diagnosis and treatment of autism* (pp. 33–52). Boston: Springer.

Fuchs, D., & Deshler, D. D. (2007). What we need to know about responsiveness to intervention (and shouldn't be afraid to ask). *Learning Disabilities Research & Practice, 22*(2), 129–136. doi:10.1111/j.1540-5826.2007.00237.x

Gehlbach, H. (2017). Learning to walk in another's shoes. *Phi Delta Kappan, 98*(6), 8–12. doi: 10.1177/0031721717696471

Gerould, L. (1996). *Balancing the tray.* Schnecksville, PA: Carbon-Lehigh Right to Education Task Force.

Glanton, T. (2019, November 9). *Successfully managing all your discipline challenges: What they did not teach you in principal school!* Presentation at the ASCD Conference on Educational Leadership, National Harbor, MD.

Grandin, T. (2008). *The way I see it: A personal look at autism and Asperger's* (4th ed.). Arlington, TX: Future Horizons.

Gray, C. (2015). *The new social story book, revised and expanded 15th anniversary edition: Over 150 social stories that teach everyday social skills to children and adults with autism and their peers.* Arlington, TX: Future Horizons.

Greene, R. W. (2014). *The explosive child: A new approach for understanding and parenting easily frustrated, chronically inflexible children.* New York: HarperCollins.

Hall, M. (2015). *Red: A crayon's Story.* New York: Greenwillow Books.

Happé, F., & Frith, U. (2006, January). The weak coherence account: Detail-focused cognitive style in autism spectrum disorders. *Journal of Autism Developmental Disorders, 36*(1), 5–25.

Henkes, K. (1991). *Chrysanthemum.* New York: Greenwillow Books.

Hudson, C. C., Hall, L., & Harkness, K. L. (2019). Prevalence of depressive disorders in individuals with autism spectrum disorder: A meta-analysis. *Journal of Abnormal Child Psychology, 47*(1), 165–175. doi: 10.1007/s10802-018-0402-1

Kaplan, S. (2017, January 10). The truth about vaccines, autism and Robert F. Kennedy Jr.'s conspiracy theory. *Washington Post.* Retrieved from https://www.washingtonpost .com/news/speaking-of-science/wp/2017/01/10/the-facts-about-vaccines-autism-and -robert-f-kennedy-jr-s-conspiracy-theory/

Knowles, J. (2012). *See you at Harry's.* Somerville, MA: Candlewick Press.

Krupp, D. R., Barnard, R. A., Duffourd, Y., Evans, S. A., Mulqueen, R. M., Bernier, R., Rivière, J. B., Fombonne, E., & O'Roak, B. J. (2017). Exonic mosaic mutations contribute risk for autism spectrum disorder. *American Journal of Human Genetics, 101*(3), 369–390. doi: /10.1016/j.ajhg.2017.07.016

Kutscher, M. L. (2004). *ADHD: Living right now!* White Plains, NY: Neurology Press.

Lynch, C. L. (2019, May 4). "It's a spectrum" doesn't mean what you think. *NeuroClastic*. Retrieved from https://neuroclastic.com/2019/05/04/its-a-spectrum-doesnt-mean-what-you-think/

Maximo, J. O., Cadena, E. J., & Kana, R. K. (2014). The implications of brain connectivity in the neuropsychology of autism. *Neuropsychology Review, 24*(1), 16–31. doi: 10.1007/s11065-014-9250-0

National Center for Learning Disabilities. (n.d.). *IDEA final regulations: Aligning IDEA and ESSA to support students with disabilities*. Retrieved from https://www.ncld.org/news/policy-and-advocacy/idea-final-regulations-aligning-idea-and-essa-to-support-students-with-disabilities

Nelson, L., & Lind, D. (2015, February 24). *The school to prison pipeline, explained*. Retrieved from http://www.justicepolicy.org/news/8775

Osborne, M. P. (2009). *Deep day in the dark sea: Magic tree house, Merlin mission*. New York: Random House Books for Young Readers.

Palacio, R. J. (2012). *Wonder*. New York: Random House.

Polimeni, M. A., Richdale, A. L., & Francis, A. J. (2005). A survey of sleep problems in autism, Asperger's disorder and typically developing children. *Journal of Intellectual Disability Research, 49*(4), 260–268. doi:10.1111/j.1365-2788.2005.00642.x

Raede, D. (2018, July 19). Defense mode: Why people with Asperger's seem stuck & shutdown so often [Blog post]. Retrieved from https://www.aspergerexperts.com/blogs/entry/25-defense-mode-why-people-with-aspergers-seem-stuck-shutdown-so-often/

Robison, J. E. (2007). *Look me in the eye: My life with Asperger's*. New York: Crown.

Schlieder, M. (2007). *With open arms: Creating school communities of support for kids with social challenges using circle of friends, extracurricular activities, and learning teams*. Shawnee Mission, KS: APC.

Tager-Flusberg, H., & Kasari, C. (2013, December). Minimally verbal school-aged children with autism spectrum disorder: The neglected end of the spectrum. *Autism Research 6*(6), 468–478. doi: 10.1002/aur.1329.

Thomas, A. (2017). *The hate u give*. New York: Balzer + Bray.

Tomchek, S., & Dunn, W. (2007, March/April). Sensory processing in children with and without autism: A comparative study using the short sensory profile *American Journal of Occupational Therapy, 61,* 190–200. Updated June 13, 2018. Retrieved from doi: 10.5014/ajot.61.2.190

U.S. Centers for Disease Control and Prevention. (2013). Final 2012 reports of nationally notifiable infectious diseases. Surveillance report: United States, 2012. *Morbidity and Mortality Weekly Report, 62*(33). Retrieved from https://www.cdc.gov/mmwr/preview/mmwrhtml/mm6233a6.htm

U.S. Department of Education. (2017). Questions and Answers (Q&A) on U. S. Supreme Court case decision *Endrew F. v. Douglas County School District Re-1*. Washington, DC: Author. Retrieved from https://sites.ed.gov/idea/questions-and-answers-qa-on-u-s-supreme-court-case-decision-endrew-f-v-douglas-county-school-district-re-1/

U.S. Department of Education, National Center for Education Statistics. (2019). *Digest of education statistics, 2017* (NCES 2018-070). Washington, DC: Author. Retrieved from https://nces.ed.gov/pubs2018/2018070.pdf

U.S. Department of Education, Office for Civil Rights. (2016, December 28). *Dear colleague letter: Restraint and seclusion of students with disabilities.* Washington, DC: Author. Retrieved from https://www2.ed.gov/about/offices/list/ocr/letters/colleague-201612 -504-restraint-seclusion-ps.pdf

U.S. Department of Education, Office for Civil Rights. (2020). *2015–2016 civil rights data collection (Data snapshot: School discipline).* Washington, DC: Author. https://www2 .ed.gov/about/offices/list/ocr/docs/crdc-discipline-snapshot.pdf

Verne, J. (1870/2010). *20,000 leagues under the sea.* New York: Signet Classics. (Original work published 1870.)

Yoder, N., & Gurke, D. (2017, August). *Social and emotional learning coaching toolkit: Keeping SEL at the center.* Washington, DC: American Institutes for Research. Retrieved from https://www.air.org/sites/default/files/downloads/report/Social-and-Emotional -Learning-SEL-Coaching-Toolkit-August-2017.pdf

Index

The letter *f* following a page number denotes a figure.

About the Author

 **Barbara Boroson** is the author of *Autism Spectrum Disorder in the Inclusive Classroom: How to Reach and Teach Students with ASD* and has worked in the field of autism education for more than 25 years in clinical, administrative, and advisory capacities. She provides professional development and consultative services nationwide to school districts and parents facilitating successful inclusion, and speaks frequently at conferences of the International Literacy Association, National School Boards Association, National Association of Elementary School Principals, National Association for the Education of Young Children, and ASCD, among others, as well as at many colleges and graduate schools.

Barbara holds an undergraduate degree in writing from Cornell University and a master's degree in social work from Columbia University. She lives just outside of New York City with her husband. They have two young-adult children and a socially reticent rescue dog, all of whom have inspired them to refine the art of x-treme, differentiated co-parenting.

Barbara welcomes feedback and questions from readers. Please visit her website at http://barbaraboroson.com, contact her at barbaraboroson@gmail.com, find her on Facebook @Barbara Boroson, ASD Support, and follow her on Twitter @ BarbaraBoroson.

Related ASCD Resources: Inclusion

At the time of publication, the following resources were available (ASCD stock numbers in parentheses):

Inclusion: The Basics, 2nd Edition (#PD11OC121M)

Building on the Strengths of Students with Special Needs: How to Move Beyond Disability Labels in the Classroom by Toby Karten (#117023)

Co-Teaching Do's, Don'ts, and Do Betters by Toby J. Karten and Wendy W. Murawski (#121013)

From Goals to Growth: Intervention and Support in Every Classroom by Lee Ann Jung (#118032)

Inclusion Do's, Don'ts, and Do Betters (Quick Reference Guide) by Toby J. Karten (#QRG116082)

Leading an Inclusive School: Access and Success for ALL Students by Richard A. Villa and Jacqueline S. Thousand (#116022)

Leading for Differentiation: Growing Teachers Who Grow Kids by Carol Ann Tomlinson and Michael Murphy (#115005)

Neurodiversity in the Classroom: Strengths-Based Strategies to Help Students with Special Needs Succeed in School and Life by Thomas Armstrong (#113017)

Teaching in Tandem: Effective Co-Teaching in the Inclusive Classroom by Joan Blednik and Gloria Lodata Wilson (#110029)

Your Students, My Students, Our Students: Rethinking Equitable and Inclusive Classrooms by Lee Ann Jung, Nancy Frey, Douglas Fisher, and Julie Kroener (#119019)

For up-to-date information about ASCD resources, go to www.ascd.org. You can search the complete archives of *Educational Leadership* at www.ascd.org/el.

ASCD myTeachSource®

Download resources from a professional learning platform with hundreds of research-based best practices and tools for your classroom at http://myteachsource.ascd.org/

For more information, send an e-mail to member@ascd.org; call 1-800-933-2723 or 703-578-9600; send a fax to 703-575-5400; or write to Information Services, ASCD, 1703 N. Beauregard St., Alexandria, VA 22311-1714 USA.